Careers in
Publishing
and
Booksellling

Careers in Publishing and Bookselling

SECOND EDITION

JUNE LINES

KOGAN PAGE
CAREERS SERIES

Acknowledgements

The author thanks all the contributors of case studies and information for their help and suggestions in the preparation of this new edition.

First published in 1983, entitled *Careers in Publishing*
Second edition 1994

Apart from any fair dealing for the purposes of research or private study, or criticism or review, as permitted under the Copyright, Designs and Patents Act, 1988, this publication may only be reproduced, stored or transmitted, in any form or by any means, with the prior permission in writing of the publishers, or in the case of reprographic reproduction in accordance with the terms of licences issued by the Copyright Licensing Agency. Enquiries concerning reproduction outside those terms should be sent to the publishers at the undermentioned address:

Kogan Page Ltd
120 Pentonville Road
London N1 9JN

© June Lines 1983, 1994

The right of June Lines to be identified as author of this work has been asserted by her in accordance with the Copyright, Designs and Patents Act 1988.

British Library Cataloguing in Publication Data

A CIP record for this book is available from the British Library.

ISBN 0-7494-1300-X

Typeset by DP Photosetting, Aylesbury, Bucks
Printed and bound in Great Britain by
Clays Ltd, St Ives plc

Contents

Introduction — 7

Part 1

1. Book Publishing — 11
General Publishing 11; Specialist Publishing 14; Changing Direction 16; Periodicals and Newspapers 17; Trade Unions 17

2. Jobs in Book Publishing — 19
Introduction 19; Editorial 19; Picture Research 26; Production 28; Design 32; Sales, Marketing and Publicity 34; Rights Manager 41; Copyright and Permissions Editor 44; Royalties Clerk 45

3. Allied Occupations and Freelance Opportunities — 47
Introduction 47; Literary Agents and Scouts 47; Publicists and Marketers 49; Editorial, Literary and Production Services 49; Indexers 50; Translators 51; Freelance Opportunities 52

4. Bookselling — 57
Introduction 57; Working in a Bookshop 58; Education and Training 59; Salary and Prospects 59; Applying for Jobs 60

Part 2

5. Training in Publishing and Bookselling — 63
Publishing 63; Introduction 63; Specific Careers 65; Degree and Postgraduate Diploma Courses 65;

BTEC/SCOTVEC Courses 67; National Vocational Qualifications 68; Short Courses 69; Correspondence Courses 74; Bookselling 75; Courses 76; Other Training Providers 78; Funding for Training 78

6. **Applying for a Job in Publishing**   81
Introduction 81; Job Advertisements 81; The Letter of Application 82; Your Curriculum Vitae 82; Telephone Application 83; The Response 83; The Interview 83; Accepting a Job 84; Contract of Employment 84; Temporary or Vacation Work 85

7. **Further Reading**   87

8. **Useful Addresses**   89

Introduction

Publishing is a profession with no specific entry qualifications. It calls for general knowledge, a good command of English, an eye for detail and a good memory. Specialist training or education such as art and design, languages, medicine, mathematics, science, technology, theology, business, teacher training or the law, will help you to enter a specialist field of publishing. So, also, will a command of non-academic subjects such as wine and food, horsemanship, gardening, crafts, mountaineering and so on.

Publishing and bookselling attract people who love books and reading. Those who envisage them as leisurely pursuits in elegant surroundings, where intellectual conversations with world-famous writers are daily occurrences, will suffer a rude shock once they enter the world of books. Publishing relies on large sales in a competitive international market, and publishers have the same objectives as any other business: to produce and sell goods at a profit. Publishing houses in the UK do not have a monopoly of English language publishing; they compete directly with publishers in all other English-speaking countries. They also compete indirectly with English language books originated in foreign countries. A successful publisher needs to combine both business sense *and* culture; those who publish good books unprofitably do not long survive.

In the UK, publishing is very much a London-based activity, so residence in or near the metropolitan area improves one's ability to get and change jobs. It is true that publishing activity goes on all over the country, particularly around the older universities, but London is still the nucleus, and likely to remain so, because of its great resources, communications and as the home of other media. Publishing is a profession in which men and women find equal opportunity;* competence and adaptability are the keys to success for both. The individual contribution counts for much, and personal quality, like personal incompetence, shows up quickly. Despite takeovers and mergers, often at an international level, new publishing houses, literary agencies and publicity companies are constantly being formed by those who have left the resulting large groups, widening the availability of careers in this field.

The main departments in publishing houses are editorial, production and design, sales, marketing and distribution.

The editorial function is the role most widely known by the outsider and it is the editorial chair to which most newcomers aspire, so this book tends to emphasise the role of the editor. In book publishing, the first three areas predominate, with the sales department connecting with publicity, marketing and distribution. Contact with the public may be made through advertisements, direct mail or high street bookshops.

Bookselling differs from other retail trades in the same way that publishing differs from other manufacturing industries: each item in stock or production is a new line for a new public. Bookshop experience is invaluable for publishers and their sales representatives.

The greatest rewards in the industry lie in the satisfaction of working with diverse and talented authors and colleagues in a job which offers responsibility and constant variety, and in the pleasure of handling the product of one's labour. Publishing is a comparatively small industry, and a very personal business.

---

* Where masculine pronouns have been used, feminine pronouns are equally applicable, and vice versa.

Part 1

Addresses of the organisations mentioned in the text are given in Chapter 8.

Please note that UK telephone area codes are due to change on 16 April 1995. Readers will need to check the numbers given in this book after that date.

Chapter 1
Book Publishing

General Publishing

General (or trade) publishing is the part of the trade with which most people are familiar. It includes fiction and non-fiction, adult and children's books, whether sold in hard covers or paperback, available from shops, through book clubs or by mail order. The books may be directly promoted by the authors through personal signing sessions at bookshops, reviewed in the press, on radio and television, turned into plays and films or serialised in newspapers and magazines.

The publishing process will often begin with the publisher or agent having an idea for a book. The publisher seeks a suitable author, who will sign a contract to write it (the author will be commissioned). An agent may organise an auction for a book with high sales potential, and then make a deal with the publisher whose offer is most favourable. Once the manuscript is accepted, the publisher will be responsible for transforming it into a finished book, usually in consultation with the author. The author may receive a lump sum for the work (an outright purchase by the publisher) but a royalty is more usual and would be insisted on by an agent. A royalty is a fixed percentage, either of the cover price for each copy of the book sold or of the publisher's net receipts, plus a share in any other deals.

Except in the field of fiction, unsolicited manuscripts – those sent in unrequested – form a very small part of publishers' output; a figure of 1 to 2 per cent a year is average.

The Hardback Edition

Hardbacks are likely to be printed on good quality paper with wide margins, perhaps generously illustrated, the pages sewn in rather than glued, and bound between boards covered by cloth or a cheaper material (paper or plastic). The whole is then enclosed by a printed jacket. Hard binding is used for books which need to last: first editions of novels, library copies, reference books, and copies for readers who want their books in a permanent form. The jackets are designed and produced by the publisher's art department, or commissioned from a freelance designer, well in advance of publication. The publicity department or editor adds a blurb (a promotional statement) about the book's contents, the author, and possibly other related titles. Jackets are sent to overseas agents to promote advance sales of the book among the trade, and the home trade representatives show copies to wholesalers and bookshops and take orders, known as subscribing the book.

Paperbacks
These account for over half of the publishing output in the UK. If a paperback publisher originates a book in preference to reprinting another's hardback, then a hardback publisher may in turn make an offer for the hardcover rights. In these circumstances, the paperback edition precedes the hardback. A hardback publisher may, however, decide to produce his own paperback edition, simultaneously or at a later date. The printed sheets may come from the same print run as the hardback edition, though possibly on cheaper paper, and they are bound up in heavy quality paper covers. The price is lower than the hardback (it reflects the cheaper binding and a lower percentage royalty for the author), the publisher sells the book through normal trade outlets, and it is known as a trade paperback.

Alternatively, the publisher may show the typescript to a mass-market paperback house in the hope that it will be found sufficiently attractive for an offer before hardback publication, though some paperbackers like to see a previous track record. In the case of a best-selling author, a paperback offer may precede delivery of the manuscript. The paperback house then pays an advance (to be set against royalty earnings) to the publisher. A sale of film or television rights in a book increases the value of all other rights. A mass-market paperback edition is newly typeset, and printed on smaller, thinner pages with narrower margins. It will possibly have less space between the lines, and often fewer illustrations than the hardback original. The cover design confirms or announces any film or television tie-in, as this makes sales leap.

Paperback titles may be sold individually to wholesalers or bookshops, or made up into packages of assorted titles. The packages are supplied on a sale or return basis, so the net sales may not be known until the returns have winged their way back to the paperback warehouse for pulping.

Children's Books
Books for young children are small format, often stiffened, possibly highly illustrated in full colour, and rather short. They may have pop-up pictures. Older children's books are usually paperbacked, many of them being classics on which royalties are no longer payable. (Royalties are paid on copyright material, and the copyright – the exclusive right to produce or control – expires 50 years after the author in UK law, or 50 years after first publication, whichever is later. The European Community is currently working on harmonisation at 70 years.) Examples of books now in the public domain are the works of Rudyard Kipling, Beatrix Potter, Frances Hodgson Burnett, Lewis Carroll, Kenneth Grahame, Hans Andersen, Edith Nesbit, Robert Louis Stevenson and Jonathan Swift (though his *Gulliver's Travels* was written as political satire). Other countries have their own laws relating to copyright, and some ignore it completely.

Book Clubs
A hardbound book club edition is sold to the club by the originating publisher, on the strength of the manuscript or proofs. Available to club members only and at a lower price than the trade edition, it may be issued with it simultaneously. The copies may be printed by the clubs if a large quantity is involved; otherwise they are taken from the trade edition print run, which enables the publisher to keep the price down. The author receives an agreed share of the net receipts from club deals. Clubs and mail order operations are increasingly buying paperback editions.

Overseas Editions
Publishers abroad are shown the book at some stage – manuscript, proof or finished copy – with a view to buying either translation rights or English language rights for their particular territories. The English language publishers (especially in the USA which is a crucial market for UK houses) will possibly buy copies from the UK run, bearing their own imprint on the cover and preliminary pages. Foreign language publishers will produce the book in their own country after they have had it translated (unless it is a co-edition – see below), reproducing illustrations

from film supplied by the originating (initiating) publisher, or buying illustration sheets to bind up with their text. The cost of translation is acknowledged in either a low advance payment, a low royalty, or both. Again, the author receives an agreed percentage of all such payments. The deal with publishers abroad will often permit them to sell other rights within their own territories, such as paperback, book club, serial rights for magazine reproduction, television and radio.

Co-editions
The originating publisher may be able to spread the cost of a heavily illustrated work over a large number of simultaneous foreign language editions, by producing such an enticing manuscript, backed up by a well-illustrated dummy of the book, that he can persuade a consortium of overseas publishers to undertake editions. They all reap the benefit of a lower unit cost resulting from the longer print run.

Some companies, 'packagers', do not themselves publish but specialise in originating and producing co-editions to sell to publishers and other distributors who may lack the resources to undertake such ambitious projects. They commission the manuscript and illustrations, organise the production and delivery, and sell the various rights; the presses start to roll when the package has been sold to enough publishers to make the project pay. It is an advantage to many publishers to be offered a virtually ready-made product; it can be slotted quickly into their programmes and boost turnover. The disadvantages include lack of control over content, reprints and subsidiary rights. Own-brand books for retailers are a development from this base.

Specialist Publishing
The titles produced by a general publisher usually reflect the interests of the founders or directors. Older companies are often large, and carry several specialist lists. New companies are constantly being formed by publishers who see an opportunity ignored by existing firms and start up on their own to bridge the gap. The smaller companies are unshackled by the high overheads of the large organisations and consequently can produce books more quickly and cheaply, and take risks that would make the larger houses shudder.

The specialist field is divided between subjects and methods.

About 200 academic and professional subjects are listed in *British Qualifications* published annually by Kogan Page; since they are all formally studied in courses, all need textbooks as well as material for background reading.

Medical books, for example, are written for trade publishing (often as family health reference books), as well as for professional purposes. They are well produced, often heavily illustrated, written by professionals for a lay readership. Other specialist subjects also published for the general public include music, theology, archaeology and cartography. Many subjects studied academically will have a greater general market.

Educational Publishers
They provide the entire range from first school readers to postgraduate studies, diversifying along the way into medicine, science, technology, law and so on. Books for schools and colleges are often written by teachers whose material has been class-tested in use. Prices must be low and publishers strive to secure adoptions, to ensure that their titles get on to the lists of set books issued by the examination boards, or at least become recommended reading. A successful textbook brings rewards for both the publisher and author over many years, the latter enjoying academic prestige as well as royalties. Books for university studies are written mainly by dons and professors, and in some subjects – art history, for example – will command respectable sales to the general public. The results of their research are written up by the specialists for their peers. The circulation will be limited (it is sometimes possible to quantify world demand to the nearest hundred copies) but such works are essential for certain top-level professionals and command high prices.

Dictionaries, Encyclopaedias and Reference Books
These publications represent considerable investment by publishers: a general editor is required for each, as well as a team of sub-editors, researchers, contributors, lexicographers, picture researchers and so on. The editorial workload is immense and carried out to a strict timetable.

Yearbooks and directories are compiled from information sources and mailed questionnaires; they are produced under high pressure, as their commercial success is heavily dependent on the speed and accuracy of their updating. Computers have simplified the storage of data and reduced the work of information retrieval and update.

Encyclopaedias or extended studies (on subjects such as war, angling, cookery or needlecraft, for example), may be produced in heavily illustrated magazine-format instalments, known as partworks, for monthly or weekly purchase from newsagents; the high cost of the entire work is less apparent when each part is sold at a comparatively modest price. However, the number of subscribers may diminish after the first enthusiasm, so the publisher's costs will rise since he is committed to completion for the remaining buyers.

Fine Art Publishing
Fine art book publishing involves the high quality reproduction of works of art, often by contemporary painters. By limiting such editions to a stated number, the publisher can enhance their value, and they may become collectors' items shortly after publication. Each plate may in fact be a very fine print, and sometimes a signed print will be incorporated in each copy. The books will be large in format, and may be sponsored by the artist's gallery. Prices are high, but less than the cost of buying the artist's prints which may not, in any case, be on the market.

Fine Bindings
Limited editions are usually provided with fine bindings. The Folio Society is unusual in that it offers its members popular titles in fine and unusual bindings at prices which benefit from the economies of quantity. Otherwise, in the trade, fine bindings are applied only to individual orders. Publishers sometimes present an author with a finely bound copy of his own work, and each runner-up for the Booker Prize is presented with a copy of his book in a fine binding.

Changing Direction

Publishers established in one specialist field may find it difficult to launch out into others except by acquiring existing lists. So if a small specialist house is up for sale, it may be snapped up by a company wishing to acquire a known imprint to extend its activities in a new direction.

However good a book on natural history might be, it could meet considerable bookseller resistance if it appeared on the list of a house hitherto known mainly for women's studies. Because it wasn't on the list of an established natural history house, booksellers would conclude that it had been rejected as below standard. Publishers reach the public through booksellers, so there is a risk of stillbirth if booksellers don't subscribe, hence the use of direct mail and the appeal of book clubs. A children's book publisher could irretrievably damage his credibility by diversifying into books on science fiction or sex.

There are always opportunities for writers, editors and illustrators in popular publishing. This includes such subjects as sports and games, food and wine, cookery, gardening, pet care, DIY, home crafts, transport, weapons – the list is endless. Increasingly, cassettes and videos are being sold with books, offering scope for people with the vision and ability to develop such packages.

Multimedia

Book publishers are increasingly exploiting the possibilities offered by electronic media: the conversion of books into a presentation combining text with image, sound, animation or video or any combination of these. CD-ROM (compact disc-read only memory) has made it possible to produce an enormous amount of mixed media on a single disc.

Periodicals and Newspapers

Periodical publishing is akin to newspapers in that the writers and editors are more likely to be trained journalists than book editors. The frequency of publication dictates short lead times, and a tendency to trivialise. Newspapers and magazines are outside the scope of this book; see *Careers in Journalism*, 6th edition, also published by Kogan Page.

Trade Unions

The basic aim of every trade union is to maintain, protect and improve its members' standard of living. The National Union of Journalists (NUJ) represents the interests of those employed in the publishing industry, creatively engaged in editorial, production, design, rights and marketing. It publishes recommended hourly rates of pay. Bookshop staff are represented by the Administrative, Clerical, Technical and Supervisory section (ACTS) of the Transport and General Workers Union.

Chapter 2
Jobs in Book Publishing

Introduction
Publishing houses differ in their organisation, but most have hree main departments: editorial, production/design and sales/marketing. Additionally, there are the service departments found in most commercial offices: accounts, reception, personnel, warehousing and distribution. Secretaries may be attached to departments but personal computers now enable more people to handle their own correspondence. Secretaries can learn the publishing job and move across into other parts of the publishing sector. At present, companies tend to be slightly understaffed to control costs. Freelance work is discussed in Chapter 3.

Editorial
More publishing recruits are attracted to this department than any other, although editors are a very small percentage of the total publishing labour force in Britain, which itself is in the order of 20,000. The other departments offer more job opportunities.

The editorial department takes the author's manuscript and, in due course, hands back a bound book; it is the department which has the most contact with the author. The work of an editor involves liaising with other departments on the design, planning and production of each book. The editor may commission the pictures or drawings and the index, read and edit the manuscript, prepare it for the typesetter, check the proofs, and be responsible for assembling all the various parts, paginated in correct order, for the printer.

Qualities Required
Editors need considerable general knowledge, should be able to

appreciate good writing, have a good command of written English including grammar, punctuation and spelling, have a retentive memory, clear handwriting and the ability to organise their own work. For the desk editor, in particular, much routine work is involved; the editor must be dedicated and accurate and able to work through constant interruptions. A commissioning editor must be imaginative, with plenty of ideas, and be aware of what is going on in the world and in the publishing industry as a whole.

Education and Training

A degree is useful (essential in specialist academic fields), but often insufficient in itself. Some companies insist on editors being graduates regardless of the work done; others show greater flexibility and appoint on the basis of general abilities. Editors in specialist subjects may also have professional qualifications, having trained in medicine, law, accountancy, the sciences and so on.

Languages, too, are important; publishing is an international business and editors frequently communicate with overseas publishers regarding co-editions and sales of rights. All editors should be able to type or use a personal computer.

Salary and Prospects

There is no automatic promotion or salary structure; in a small company there may be no room for promotion, and the only way to move up will be to move out. In larger companies promotion is often preferred to bringing in new people as this saves on training and recruitment.

The salary for editorial assistants ranges from £7,500 to £12,000; commissioning editors can expect £15,000 to £25,000. The highest editorial salaries are paid to those who specialise in science, medicine and technology. These salaries are paid for performance, which is measured by individual editors' book revenue (new and reprints), the number of titles produced, contribution to company profit, quality of the product, and the ability to acquire and retain authors, top-level advisers and consultants.

Benefits may include extra medical insurance, company pensions, company cars, interest-free loans for season tickets and generous maternity or paternity leave. Holidays usually range from four to six weeks. Most publishing staff can buy their own company's books at a discount, and a trade discount is allowed between publishers.

The chart on page 22 shows the chronological order of selected stages in book production; the terms can be related to the job descriptions which follow.

Editorial Functions

The editorial function is divided between acquiring the manuscripts and preparing them for publication. The *acquisitions* or *commissioning editor* (also known as sponsoring editor or publisher) is the list builder, whose main task is to find authors and books of quality. He needs to have an instinct about which books will sell as there are no foolproof market survey techniques. He will not necessarily have worked his way through the department, but could have been engaged because of his specialist knowledge and good contacts with potential authors. He will probably have editorial training, but may also have desk-editing back-up in house. The editor is always alert for sales possibilities for his new titles, and constantly looks for new ways to expand the market. He may be involved in buying rights to republish titles already issued by another UK house, an overseas English language publisher, or a foreign language publisher. He will commission translations of foreign titles and be competent to check them, or find readers who can. He needs to find new writers, see potential in untried work, encourage writers who are going through an unproductive or difficult period, and retain authors who look like wandering towards rival houses. He negotiates and makes contacts with literary agents, keeping up these connections to make sure their good offerings come to him. He originates large projects and sets up a team to carry them through.

The editors have the closest contact with authors; they need to read widely and be aware of buying trends and current events. In liaison with other departments, the editor takes the accepted manuscript through the various stages to deliver a bound book within a given time at an agreed price. Within these constraints, editors always work to deadlines, and stress is an occupational hazard.

The top position is the *editorial director*; this means a seat on the board and overall control of the department. Some houses have a *managing editor*, combining the roles of manager and editor. He may run a centralised copy-editing department, and commission and supervise freelance editorial workers. This role

Different stages in the production of a book

Editorial Department	Production/Design Department	Sales/Marketing/Distribution	Payments made by Publisher
Book proposal. Editor confirms author. →		Positive sales reaction. Decision to proceed.	
Contract agreed with author and signed. →	Specification prepared; project estimated.	Author questionnaire sent to author and returned. Advance information sheet prepared.	Payment to author on signature of contract.
Picture list in from author. Picture research starts. →			
Manuscript received from author. →		Jacket/cover copy drafted.	
Expert reading of manuscript. →			
Manuscript accepted. Pictures in or .... →	Illustrations commissioned.		Payment made to author on acceptance of manuscript.
Typescript edited. →	Edited typescript to design. Project re-estimated. Edited typescript marked up and draft layout made.	Manuscript and pictures sent to book clubs, overseas publishers, paperback houses, etc.	

Jobs in Book Publishing 23

Proofs to author and editor for correction. Corrections incorporated, proofs back to production.	Typescript set; pictures originated. Production scheduled. Jackets printed.	Jackets and advance information sheets sent out. Advertising and publicity plans made.
	Layout made of text and pictures combined.	Title subscribed by home sales reps and overseas agents.
Index commissioned. →	Corrections proofed. Picture captions set. Pictures imposed on text sheets.	
Editor corrects new proofs. Index delivered, edited and sent to printer. →	Index set; all final corrections proofed. Final estimate. Printing starts.	Any other English language editions confirmed ready for printing (US, book club).
	→ Binding	Advertising and publicity.
Editor approves running sheets. ↘	→ Delivery to warehouse.	Despatch of orders, review and inspection copies.
		Publicity machine revs up.
		Publication.
		Payment due on publication made to author, picture sources, etc.

embraces a large planning and business element, and calls for a good understanding of editorial routines. He is measured by his ability to deliver the books by the scheduled date.

The editor also reads and reports on commissioned and unsolicited manuscripts and proposals, but readers are also employed. Commissioned manuscripts usually proceed to publication with few problems, but some need remedial attention (a delicate matter of negotiation between editor and author). Comparatively few unsolicited manuscripts are accepted for publication, but they all have to be read and assessed; the editor must be alert for their merits, which may be well concealed. Most editors can point to best sellers on other publishers' lists which they themselves had previously turned down. It does not automatically follow that the decisions were wrong: manuscripts are frequently offered to publishers who are unsuitable for the material – it is a waste of time and postage to send fiction to a non-fiction house, for example. But an editor may appreciate the quality of the writing while realising that the book, as submitted, has grave faults which could be put right if the author would accept suggestions and be guided. This all requires care and time, in the midst of a busy schedule, and is a peripheral task as against the need to process accepted manuscripts which will recover investment more quickly.

The editor works with a minimum of supervision. He may draft contracts and formal agreements, accept and reject manuscripts, be responsible for maintaining his own deadlines and budgets, pass page proofs for production after checking all the last details, draft and/or approve jacket copy, catalogue copy, and advance information sheets and make presentations of his books to the sales representatives at seasonal conferences.

The *desk editor* (also known as a sub-editor, or copy editor) spends most of his time at his desk, supervised by and responsible to a senior. He reads a manuscript, checks it for copyright illustrations or passages, and prepares it for the printer by ensuring consistency of content and style. He checks references and facts (when he has doubts), and corrects the grammar, spelling and punctuation. He may discuss with, or suggest to, the author revisions, picture content, design and production schedules; choose the illustrations, and draft the jacket blurb and catalogue copy. Once the manuscript has been edited, it will be designed ready for production. When the text has been set in type, the editor sends proofs to the author, proof-reads one set himself, collates the two sets of corrections, and then returns the proofs to the printer (via the production department) for correction and the next stage of production. Books without illustrations are usually typeset directly into pages; books with integrated illustrations, tabular matter or complicated make-up may have several proofing stages (galleys, montage proofs and page proofs), although much of this work is simplified by the use of computer design or desk-top systems.

The desk editor may also be responsible for compiling or updating entries for directories and encyclopaedias from data supplied. In a small company, he is often involved with other departments; in a large company, he may be in a centralised copy-editing department and rarely move outside it.

An *editorial assistant* is the beginner in the department, and will probably have keyboard skills at least. He works under the guidance of a senior on tasks such as desk editing, the preparation of captions for illustrations, listing of illustrations, chronologies, bibliographies, listing names to appear on maps and diagrams for the cartographer or artist to work from, checking indexes, researching bilbiographical information, updating books for new editions, doing snippets of translation, obtaining pictures and so on.

Paperback and Book Club Editors
If the company is mainly concerned with buying rights in the finished product of a hardback publisher, the editor will be particularly involved in evaluating the suitability of works for the company list. When the work is first submitted in manuscript form by the originating publisher, the editor is free to suggest changes to the text, the design, illustrations or cover which would make the book more acceptable. The editor may negotiate the contract terms with the first publisher.

When paperback houses originate their own titles, and produce their own editions of bought-in works, their editorial departments work on orthodox lines. A book club wishing to originate works will generally arrange for a packaging publisher to undertake the editorial side.

Case Study
Jimmy works as an editor with special responsibility for gathering information.

> I read microbiology at university. After graduating I applied to many of the specialist science publishers. I was unsuccessful in all my

attempts to gain a position in editorial – the main reason being lack of experience. Therefore I attended the London College of Printing where I did a postgraduate diploma in printing and publishing studies. This provided me with some insight into publishing/printing practices and, I hoped, a better chance of obtaining an editorial position.

After a few months working with a small publisher as a production assistant, I became sub-editor with a large international publisher of medical books and journals. As journals sub-editor I was responsible for the total production of three specialist biological journals. Besides editorial duties my work involved liaison between editorial boards and authors, commissioning of artwork and much contact with printers. The job gave me a thorough grounding in the processing and production of titles from original manuscript to finished article. I continued in this position for about three years by which time the job had become less demanding – the problems arising were becoming more repetitive and less challenging as I was becoming familiar with how to solve them. I felt that I might benefit by finding a position involving different aspects of publishing practice, possibly on book production.

I am presently employed as an editor with a medium-sized book publisher. Here I have special responsibility for gathering information for use in directories and my duties can vary according to the type of book involved. New titles, for instance, involve lengthy discussions with consultants and formulation of the contents and format. Information is gathered from a variety of sources: mailings, public services or by using computer-search facilities. My experience is useful when the information has been compiled and the manuscript is to be edited and prepared for printing. I am finding that there are now new challenges and ample problems to be solved!

Picture Research

Picture research is a professional wing of the editorial or art department in those companies which publish illustrated books. Researchers are predominantly women. The researcher will be provided with a list of pictures or subjects which are needed for a book, or she will be given a copy of the manuscript, briefed on the format and design, and then asked to provide an agreed number of suitable photographs. In either case she works to a budget (therefore she must know the cost of a print, the charge for its retention in case a decision is not made within the 'free' period, and the cost of reproduction charged by the copyright holder), and a deadline (she must be familiar with worldwide sources and the time they take to supply prints). A knowledge of copyright relating to illustrations will be acquired, as well as the equally essential but prosaic documentation routines attached to picture reproduction. Picture researchers need to reconcile the editor's insistence on high quality with the budget for the book, and cope with conflicting (and possibly preconceived) ideas of author and editor about what should be included.

Some months may be allocated for the acquisition of illustrations, as the picture list can often be prepared well before delivery of the manuscript; this enables the researcher to work on a subject in depth over a long period. The deadlines on partworks and periodicals are much shorter, so the work is inevitably more superficial unless the researcher has made a speciality of the subject matter.

Publishing houses build up their own picture archives; these are often extensive, and familiarisation is an essential part of learning the job. The archives are a business asset which can be exploited.

Education and Personal Qualities
Entry into picture research may take place at all educational levels, but usually a degree, with an emphasis on art history, art training, history, science and languages is required. Any expert knowledge is useful, since pictures are required for all subjects. Fluency in a foreign language is valuable, especially when dealing with foreign picture sources over the telephone. A good telephone manner is essential, to inspire the picture source at the other end of the line with confidence in the loan of material, or the interest to search it out. One must be able to deal with correspondence and secretarial entry to picture research happens occasionally. Personal qualities include curiosity, tenacity, imagination, visual awareness and versatility. The researcher has to be punctilious about details and good at dealing with people – negotiation and persuasion form a large part of the job.

Training
There is no formal pre-entry training; previous experience in a library, gallery or museum is useful. The job may be learned by on-the-job experience in a picture library or publishing house, where there will be the opportunity to research on many different subjects as well as learning from colleagues. The researcher must acquire a knowledge of picture sources worldwide by studying, for example, museum and library catalogues,

directories and guide books to stately homes. Copyright knowledge is vital, and is usually acquired on the job, together with documentation requirements for the loan and reproduction of pictures. Courses are listed in Chapter 5.

Salary and Prospects
Salaries start at around £8,500 to £11,000. There are few chances of promotion; it is more a question of changing one's job, if there is no possibility of managing the section, in favour of magazines or television. See Chapter 3 for freelance opportunities.

Case Study
Martin, a picture research manager, left school at 17, and after nine months as a civil service clerk, applied for a place in a local art school.

> I spent three years there, with textile design as my main subject; I also studied etching. On leaving, I applied for a job as a picture researcher with a partwork company, and was offered it. I enjoyed this very much but was, unfortunately, made redundant. After a few months of freelancing, I went to the *Reader's Digest* book division as a freelance 'fill-in', and twenty years later I'm still there, as picture research manager. When I joined, there was no centralised picture research department; I automatically set up records while doing research and, in fact, founded the archive. I am now responsible for supplying all stock pictures for our books and for picture rights.

Production

The production department is responsible for the manufacture of the books; its function is to ensure that books are produced to the highest standard available for the agreed price, and within a specified time. Designers may be under editorial supervision, but are usually attached to the production department, with their own manager or director.

Production Controller
In larger companies, there are several teams, each consisting of an editor, designer, production controller, and sometimes a picture researcher, and each team works on its own series or list of titles. The team works together to ensure a smooth and efficient flow. The page size, design, style and printing process of each book will have been agreed by the team, probably at

contract stage, when a rough estimate would have been prepared to confirm the financial soundness of the project.

On delivery, a manuscript is cast off (a word count is made) to check that the author has delivered roughly the agreed length. The production controller draws up an accurate specification for the book and uses his expert knowledge of typesetters, printers, paper suppliers and binders to decide which companies should be invited to estimate for the work. Some publishers will have agreements to channel much of their work through specified suppliers, thereby simplifying the estimating process.

He sets out the favourable prices on a standard form, together with the known in-house expenses such as illustrations, permission fees and index, then adds enough to cover correction charges, wage increases during the lead time, and contingencies, and finally produces his own estimate for differing quantities. The editor uses the completed form to estimate the cover price (the price paid by the bookshop customer) by adding a mark-up for trade discounts, the publisher's gross profit, and the author's royalty. If the resultant figure is too high, the team discusses cost reductions. Savings can be achieved by reducing the quality of production, changing the design, cutting the text or reducing the number of illustrations to shorten the extent.

The production controller places orders for typesetting, machining (printing) and binding, as well as purchasing paper and binding materials, involving many different companies; he ensures that all the production stages, both inside and outside the house, are carried out to the required standard and on schedule (to meet delivery dates required for the Christmas market, the school year, a special exhibition or event, and so on). He must also check actual costs against estimates when the work is done.

When manufacture is carried out abroad, the production controller deals with foreign suppliers - a knowledge of other languages is valuable - and he needs to allow for fluctuations in exchange rates when payments are due. He will also establish good relations with freight forwarders and shippers if there is no shipping manager. Since his department spends more than any other in the company (millions of pounds a year in large companies), he needs to have financial acumen, technical knowledge, and the ability to administer and organise efficiently.

Production Director (or Manager)
The production director will be on the board of directors; his role

is crucial to the company's efficiency and profitability, and carries considerable financial responsibility. He will have been a production controller earlier in his career, and show excellent administrative, numerical and bargaining skills. He rarely works on specific titles, but is a policy maker, extending the company's contacts with the printing industry worldwide to ensure he is getting the best deals.

Production Assistant
This flexible description often covers someone who has entered publishing in a trainee capacity, or as a secretary, designer or stock controller, and then decides to train for production at evening or day-release classes, while doing fairly undemanding production work on the job. He may be given responsibility for leaflets or straightforward reprints to start with, or for archiving the illustration originations held by different printers for the company, moving up when training or experience make him eligible.

Book Jackets and Covers
These are often the responsibility of one production executive. Information is provided by the editor, who may draft the preliminary text (called 'copy'). The blurb is the promotional passage which 'sells' the book to the reader, and is polished by the publicity department. A rough design is prepared and, when approved, worked up into a full-sized piece of artwork. Freelance designers are frequently engaged for this work; paperback houses in particular need a large number of covers for a wide variety of subjects. The text is added once the artwork is approved. The production of jackets (for hardbound books) and covers (for paperbacks) involves colour work, even for publishing houses which produce only monochrome books.

Book Clubs
They may have a large production element engaged in the mass reprinting of existing books. In the largest, the volume of work exceeds that of most publishers.

Education and Training
Preliminary training (see Chapter 5) is necessary for both production and design; production staff often move from the printing industry into publishing, after taking a London School of Printing course.

Salary and Prospects

Salaries for production staff usually start higher than those for editors: from £12,000 to £14,000 for a well-trained worker who has taken an approved course. A production controller can expect £12,000 upwards. Production editors straddle two roles; they have similar functions to a managing editor, but on a smaller scale.

Institutes tend to have one person who does everything. Publishing/production departments have opportunities for lower-level entry, with starting salaries from £8,000 to £10,000. The same benefits apply as for editors (page 20).

The production manager/director runs the department, and his second in command is the natural successor. Promotion often lies in moving to another company. The production manager of a large, thriving company with considerable turnover may earn up to £50,000.

Case Study

Peter is the Production Manager for a non-fiction book publisher.

> I was a 'university drop-out', and so I had some time to spend finding out what I wanted to do. Fortunately, a friend worked in an advertising agency and got me some copywriting work 'on the side', and I also picked up a regular writing spot with a couple of magazines.
>
> At the time, I was thinking more of journalism as a career, but I also found myself interested in the actual processes that words take in their route to publication. So, after a while, I felt that I wanted to find out more, and it was a happy coincidence that there was a local polytechnic offering a full-time diploma course in publishing.
>
> I found the course remarkably stimulating. There were subjects on the curriculum to suit most tastes, and I think most students rapidly began to adopt a professional attitude. Personally, I enjoyed the practical project work most – being able to use their typesetting equipment and the process studio was great fun.
>
> My first job was as a desk editor with a professional institution, in London. They were very impressed with my qualification. I was impressed that they were impressed. I was tasked with editing, proof-reading, and administering a learned journal and academic textbooks. The first few months were quite difficult – high workloads and periodical deadlines were new to me and it took a while to get to grips with, particularly when I got the job because I was supposed to know what I was doing. Also, I found London a bit difficult to get to grips with after a life in the northern counties! With time, it became easier, and the money was good. It didn't take long before I realised I was

bored with the work and uncomfortable with a highly inflexible workplace.

From what I've seen, most 'institutional' publishing tends to be the same: relatively well-paid, good benefits, dull working environment, repetitive and dull work (unless, of course, the subject is your 'bent'). Definitely something to stay away from unless you are qualified in the subject area and lean towards the academic, need the money, or don't really care about your job.

From there, I went to the publications department of a large training organisation, as a production editor (this is a good example of ambiguity in publishing job terms; in this case, it literally meant someone who was both a project editor and a production controller). The organisation was full of good ideas, and the department was a lively, happy family. I handled projects, ranging from books to video packages from start to finish, including negotiating with the suppliers, doing the costings, and so on. I relished the responsibility and the variety. After a while I was promoted to production controller, in charge of all print-buying, stocks, and so on. During this period I also got quite involved with the London publishing 'scene'. I didn't know anyone at that time who was not working in publishing, though, to be honest, I don't think this was particularly beneficial – the 'society' tends to be competitive and expensive to keep up with.

My next change came as something of a surprise, as I wasn't really looking for a new job (some would say this is the best way of finding the right one). An advert for a production controller with a book publisher in the shires was pointed out to me. A great deal of the subject matter coincided with interests of mine, and I fancied a move to the country! It was a difficult move, staying in lodgings for the first month or so, and quite expensive. The job was also a handful, as I was very much on my own and there was stuff everywhere. It's ok now though. The company has moved to larger premises, there is more than one production person, and I now spend quite a lot of time involved with forward planning. I particularly enjoy being able to communicate with the other departments on an equal footing. After all, they do say that's what successful business is all about!

Design

Duties of the design department vary according to the type of publishing company, and the way in which it is organised. The work involves all aspects of book design – layout, fount (typeface), type sizes, spacing, style and arrangement of illustrations, jacket or cover. The design must be within the limitations of available production services and acceptable costs. The department's work also includes the preparation of layouts, sketches, specimen pages and dummies, and sometimes the marking up of manuscripts for the typesetter after they have been edited. Here they will give instructions for the typesetter as to fount, type size, spacing and measure, having checked the word count and illustration list against first estimates. Where galley proofs are still used, the design department pastes up the proofed material into pages, once the proofs have been read and the artwork checked.

The *design manager* or *director* oversees all these activities. He discusses illustrated or complicated books with the author and editor in order to give visual expression to their ideas, and tries to reconcile these with the requirements of the production and sales departments. He commissions freelance artwork, or arranges the in-house preparation of artwork for illustrations, covers, publicity material, catalogues and company stationery, and imposes a visual style on the company product. The design manager needs organising and numerical ability, as well as all the qualities of a first class designer.

For specialist publishers, a designer will need to work on texts incorporating mathematical and scientific formulae, music, and so on.

Education and Training
Most designers have undertaken art and design courses (see Chapter 6); those who plan to enter publishing should ensure that their courses have a large typographical element. Illustration is almost entirely commissioned from freelances, and is less relevant to publishing than typography and graphics.

The Chartered Society of Designers is concerned with standards of competence, professional conduct and integrity. Professional designers are eligible for membership and the Society holds periodic 'portfolio surgeries' for its members, at which professionals offer advice and direction on a voluntary basis; a register is maintained by the Society which keeps a visible record of members' works.

Salary and Prospects
Salaries are low because of the over-supply of art students looking for jobs, with a starting range of £8,000 to £10,000.

There are the usual promotional chances within a large department but, after a certain point, it means moving to another company or to a different medium (for example, advertising, periodicals or television, all of which pay more – but they are more precarious). Some publishers get by with one or two designers only. One works on catalogues, leaflets and all promotional material, and the other concentrates on producing a basic format to which all the production must conform; this position offers little scope for original work. See page 54 for freelance opportunities.

Case Studies
Richard is a designer for a leading art publisher.

> After failing my first year dental exams, I decided that I was destined for publishing. I wrote off to about 12 firms in the medical/scientific field and was shortlisted for a rep's job with a medical publisher, but got no further. My first job in 'literature' was driving Dillons' van, taking educational books around to teacher training colleges.
>
> I then obtained a job as a production trainee in a publishing house where my work involved doing simple reprints, working on publicity material, occasionally buying paper and doing similar undemanding jobs. During this time I attended a day-release course one day a week, and I was also sent to a printer's for a week where I spent a day in each department, watching and asking questions. Eventually, I took on more complex book production.
>
> At one time I resigned to write music, working in a bookshop when I ran short of money, but returned to publishing after six months – this time as a designer. My only formal design training was the typography element of my day-release course, but I had been learning constantly during my time in production. I went through a probationary period and now design covers and make layouts of heavily illustrated books.

Judith is a freelance designer working for various publishers.

> I took a graphic design course at Brighton where most of my time was spent in drawing – I learned little about typography. During one vacation I worked with an art book publisher, doing paste-ups ready for the Frankfurt Book Fair. On the strength of this work, I was offered a design post when my course ended. After three years I felt it was time to move on, but it was not a happy decision because, in my new firm, my lack of typographical training was a handicap, and I left. Now I am doing well as a freelance designer.

Sales, Marketing and Publicity

The main function of the sales department is to sell books and rights. To this end, its marketing and publicity sections are responsible for the pre-publication research, preparation, appearance and despatch of catalogues, price-lists, leaflets, posters, display stands, and all other sales aids. They are also responsible for advertising and promotion of the product, for sending out review copies and wringing the last drop of (preferably free) publicity from any reviews, news items or events. This work involves liaison with editorial, production and design.

Sales Department
This section keeps records of sales and customers, and works with the accounts department checking creditworthiness and credit control; it monitors dues (orders in advance of publication), stock levels, details of volume sales and so on. The sales department is heavily staffed. No matter how good the books are, if they do not reach the customer and translate into revenue, everything has been a waste of time. The sales person plays a crucial role in company cash flow.

Sales Director
He runs the sales department; he may be personally involved in all aspects of the business, or take complete control of one side only – export, for example – leaving other areas to managers. He should have a thorough knowledge of the trade, both in the home and export markets; he may have been an agent or representative, or have worked in an editorial capacity. Home sales include those to wholesalers and bookshop chains with central buying arrangements, book clubs, special edition sales (carrying the imprint of another company – sometimes a non-publisher), and big rights deals involving paperbacking or serialisation.

Home Sales Representative
He usually works from home; he is a car driver and is physically fit. The rep has a defined territory and arranges weekly itineraries so that all his customers receive periodic visits. He subscribes new titles and takes repeat orders, sorting out problems of supply and servicing as he goes. He carries advance jackets, specimen pages, advance information sheets and, eventually, a copy of the bound book to show bookshop buyers. At busy times, such as the start of the academic year and at Christmas, the rep will carry stock in his car to speed deliveries.

Some representatives build up such a rapport with bookshops that managers will accept their advice on ordering; a wise rep will hint to the manager when he is likely to be overstocked as well as under-supplied; though his sales manager may not appreciate the former, it can pay off in the long run. Many bookshop managers are owners too, so their profit margins and cash flow are matters of personal survival. The rep suggests, negotiates and arranges window displays. He is expected to keep his eyes open for new sales or publishing opportunities, rival activities and for early signs of financial failure, so that credit can be stopped.

Small publishing houses may share a sales force, and the reps will carry consolidated or separate lists. A sales rep may have to organise periodic presentations of new titles to local booksellers at a hotel or in a college. Big publishers hold seasonal sales conferences where reps can meet head office sales and editorial staff, and commissioning editors make a presentation of their new season's offerings, giving tips for sales and promotion. Such conferences may take the form of a resort jamboree, and be the only meetings between those who commission books and those who present them to the bookshop. In fact, bookshop experience is very useful for a representative, and some companies regard it as essential. Reps are responsible to a manager or the sales director; they are taken round by their manager or predecessor on their first few visits to familiarise themselves with their terrain and customers. All visits are recorded and reported back weekly to head office, where performance is monitored.

All reps need to be self-starters with financial ability. They also need to be fairly extrovert, persuasive, confident, adaptable, and be able to organise their own business lives with little supervision. The better they know their stock, the more efficient they will be at selling it. They will not necessarily have started in bookselling, but may have switched from another product. Naturally, they also need a clean driving licence.

Educational Representative
The educational representative calls on schools, colleges and university bookshops. He organises exhibitions of educational books at teachers' conferences during weekends or academic holidays. Educational reps are often recruited from teachers and graduates who will have an understanding of academic and instructional books, teaching methods and requirements.

Reps will record their visits, making notes of those members of staff seen, books requested for inspection, comments made, and feed back information useful to the editorial department, such as news of impending syllabus changes, organisational changes, new examination or occupational training requirements which will affect the future book needs of the establishment. On his visits to schools, the rep will discuss proposed books with staff to gauge interest, possibly arrange class validation of a textbook in preparation, find out whether the staff are themselves writing books suitable for publication, and take note of criticisms so that they can be dealt with before harm is done. Educational reps need organising ability and social graces to gain appointments with schools and colleges in the first place, and later, to ensure that they are not dismissed with their display to a dark and draughty corridor unfrequented by the people they wish to see. They get to know reps from other educational publishers by meeting them in schools and colleges. This gives them the opportunity to examine rival displays and report back to their publishers the teachers' opinions of the rival product.

During academic holidays, reps may visit summer schools. They will also have to cover for trade colleagues who are on holiday.

Export Sales
Sales for export, either direct or through UK wholesalers, account for around one-fifth of publishers' output, quite apart from the sale of rights abroad, which produces royalty income. English language sales abroad are particularly important to the health of the trade; in certain subject areas, if a book is not suitable for the US market, a UK publisher might decide not to take it on. Unless the territory is near enough to be covered from home, publishers will have an agent in those countries that import English language books. The agent holds stock, and is in business as a wholesaler or publisher, with his own army of representatives travelling to the bookshops, schools and colleges. Overseas agents often employ staff recruited from UK publishers because they know the product and have an intimate knowledge of the trade. The recruits need to acquire, if they have not already done so, a knowledge of the local conditions and language.

International Manager. He is based in the UK office and makes periodic visits to agents abroad – half the year may be spent travelling – taking news and material about new books, negotiating orders, dealing with any problems of import, payment or distribution, and possibly scouting for new ideas and authors. He also checks continually the latest trends so that the list can be adapted to harmonise with local requirements. He travels to overseas book fairs where publishers of the world gather, and receives visitors from abroad throughout the year. He may have responsibility for one specific area, such as the Caribbean, will visit it regularly and know it well.

Good health, strength and stamina are essential attributes; languages are indispensable in non-English speaking territories. One point worth remembering is that a genial personality will overcome many problems.

Education and Training
The majority of those recruited for the sales department are graduates, but anyone with a good educational background, persuasive personality, numeracy and an ability for languages, has an excellent start. Training is provided by the company in the first instance, followed by in-service courses (see Chapter 5).

Salary and Prospects
Sales representatives can start as publishing house trainees earning anything between £12,000 and £17,000 a year; a car is often supplied by the house. In-house sales managers may draw a salary ranging from £8,000 to £12,000; above that, it is a matter of negotiation based on personal qualities and the level of sales achieved. It is also possible to work for an independent company which represents publishers at home and abroad. Those working in Continental Europe will often be language graduates.

There are good prospects within a large company, especially one with overseas connections, provided one is prepared to be away from home for around six months of the year. Representatives are often promoted to managerial level, and so on to the top. Even when times are hard, companies are reluctant to reduce sales staff.

Domestic reps may be able to live in a cheap area, yet be paid on the London scale. A company car is the first benefit over one's salary, and an allowance is paid for meals and overnight stops away from home, so a good standard of living can be enjoyed. However, loss of one's driving licence is usually accompanied by loss of the job. Provided they achieve the sales, reps can adapt their routines to suit themselves, but promotion to the top jobs might mean relocation to the company office.

Freelance reps receive commission on sales and possibly a contribution towards overheads. There is no regular salary - payment is strictly dependent on results.

Case Study
Keith is a sales representative in London for a business publisher.

> I took a degree in the humanities and wanted to get into publishing; my direct approaches failed to produce a job and bookselling was the next best option. I started at Sherratt and Hughes in Slough, a bookshop and library supplier, and learned the basic skills. In bookshops you meet lots of sales reps and compare their techniques. Some are highly organised and efficient; others are hopelessly chaotic and you wonder how they get any orders. You also assess the publishers: their lists, sales material, delivery record and paperwork. Efficient publishers make a bookseller's work very much easier. Many useful contacts and friendships can be made in the bookshops.
>
> My next move was to Dillons in Gower Street, London, a superb shop with very knowledgeable staff. I started in the travel department, and moved on to the earth/life sciences department. When Gower Street personnel helped to set up Dillons in Oxford, I was invited to go there as floor manager. It was a wonderful opportunity to be in at the start of a new venture.
>
> My interest in travel books led me to start repping for a publisher specialising in the subject; my territory was London and the home counties; I stayed with them for two years before switching to Harrap, for whom I repped travel guides and dictionaries in West London until they went out of business. When two of the directors set up a marketing company which specialised in imports of art, travel and reference books, I was offered a job with them.
>
> Currently, I am repping in London for a business books publisher which also has a general non-fiction trade list and a subsidiary publishing environmental topics. Often I am selling books to my former colleagues who have stayed in bookselling, and constantly meet those who, like me, have moved into sales.
>
> Each time I change job it's important for me to look for new experiences and I always hope to find my ideal niche with the right publisher.

Publicity and Marketing
Margins in publishing are too low for regular advertising of each individual title, so there is a heavy reliance on free editorial coverage in the media arising from reviews, press releases, literary prizes, interviews, phone-ins and authors' bookshop signing sessions. All this, together with the planning, preparing and circulation of routine information about forthcoming books, is the responsibility of the publicity and marketing sides of the sales department.

The staff plan and budget for all sorts of activities including stands at exhibitions and fairs. They prepare advance information sheets, catalogues, jackets and covers, posters and leaflets; they place press advertising, organise special promotional events and special bookshop window displays. Research on how to reach the book buyer is continual; the publisher has to reach the book trade *and* the book-buying public, and must get the publicity balance right. The catalogue must be assembled at the correct time to gain the maximum advantage from mailings and export issues of the *Bookseller*. The marketing staff build up a direct mailing list, especially for specialist titles, for customers in remote areas, and for titles unlikely to be stocked by high street bookshops.

Education and Training
Recruits to the department need to be creative, able to write lively and informative copy in good English, and have a talent for public relations; a good telephone manner is essential. Graduates are often recruited straight from university for this work, but positions are also advertised. A network of good contacts has to be built up, and made the most of. Training is on the job, and by post-entry courses; the Chartered Institute of Marketing exams lead to professional qualifications (see *Careers in Marketing, Advertising and Public Relations*, 5th edition, Kogan Page).

Salary and Prospects
Salaries start between £8,000 and £11,000, depending on the company, the work required of the entrant, and the amount of training involved.

Publicity departments may be small and offer little scope for promotion. Staff often move into other publishing areas such as sales, rights and agency work (see also Chapter 3).

Case Study
Bruno is Manager of a directory publishing department within a multi-media company.

> My publishing life started after an inauspicious showing as an Oxbridge student. I landed a marketing executive job with a major magazine publisher, in its trade and retail sector. Mostly this involved a lot of canvassing and surveying on the circulation front, and a great deal of leg work. It was an eye-opener into the reality of commercial life, and very enjoyable. Sorry to say, the recession started to bite, and many titles started to fade away. In the end, the head office decided to pull the plug and the division was closed down.

I was fortunate to find another place with a smaller company, in a similar position. Things became more interesting when I was promoted to manager of circulation with the launch of a new magazine. Things began to look horrible again when the new title failed to make headway in a tough world. It closed after about six weeks. I was then offered an internal position as manager of a newly acquired list of directories, which is where I have been since. It's a small operation, but there are a couple of major titles which produce a lot of revenue and are very highly thought of.

My task is to co-ordinate the activities of the department, identify ways of improving sales and the products themselves, find opportunities for new titles, and 'figurehead' the department within the company, not to mention handling the finances. It may sound like little, but it's one heck of a job, particularly in personnel management and politics. I've been fortunate in that the company has funded me in several management courses, which have helped a great deal in widening the perspectives – you soon realise that the problems you face are not unique, and have solutions. The department has been through some tough times, and I'm looking forward to managing in the good times as well.

Rights Manager

The rights manager sells to other companies the subsidiary rights of a book which are spelt out in the publishing contract, other than those reserved by an author's agent. They include:

- English language rights, allowing the publisher's edition to be reproduced elsewhere.
- US rights, or the sale of an edition to a US publisher.
- Paperback, book club or digest editions.
- Serial rights – reproduction in a newspaper or magazine, possibly in instalments; the price is higher for serialisation in advance of publication.
- Anthology and digest rights.
- Reprint rights.
- Translation; to safeguard the integrity of the book, an author or publisher may insist on vetting the translation before it is published.
- Commercial or merchandising rights – the use of some aspect of a book in a commercial context – clothes, toiletries, greetings cards, calendars, comic strips and so on.
- Sound, radio and recording rights.
- Film, television and video rights, which can be grouped as

dramatisation; these rights and sound and commercial rights are most commonly reserved by an author's agent.
- Mechanical reproduction rights, such as photocopying, microfilm, tape and video cassettes.
- Electronic and software publishing rights.
- Reprographic reproduction rights: this is more of a preventive clause to stop unauthorised copying of a work; the same sentiment is often differently expressed in the copyright notice.

The proceeds from all these sales are shared with the authors under the terms of the publishing contract.

The work is done by post, telephone and in person, by travelling abroad to visit other publishers and book fairs, receiving visits from overseas publishers at home and by negotiating with agents and opposite numbers in other UK houses. The rights manager is attached to the sales or editorial department. He needs all the marketing skills – persuasion, negotiation, numeracy, knowledge of contracts and copyright, and languages are useful. The rights manager keeps accurate records of options granted and sales made, and informs all the departments and authors of any deals. He sends catalogues to all his contacts, which involves constant updating of records, and notifies all those concerned of any market restrictions arising from his sales.

Education and Training
There are no specific educational requirements. One usually moves into the job from another position within the house, learning by doing it as well as attending courses, and building up contacts over the years. It is a field in which women have been particularly successful; several have started in publishing as editorial assistants or secretaries, and learned the job from the beginning. In small or medium-sized houses, the rights manager also deals with copyrights and permissions (see below). When rights vacancies are advertised, an experienced person is usually required.

Salary and Prospects
The rights manager is unique; her salary and status are greatly dependent on her expertise and personality. A large income can be made for a company from rights deals, and a reward

commensurate with achievement can be expected. Rights managers sometimes move into agenting (see Chapter 3).

Case Study
Hilary is Rights Manager for a London-based packager/publisher.

I first started in design – at least, that was my college qualification, graphic design. Being born and brought up in the Home Counties, it was a relatively easy thing to move to London in search of a design career. Unfortunately, it wasn't *that* easy, and I soon needed a job of any sort simply to get some money coming in.

Via an agency, I found a position as secretary in a small packaging company, specialising in children's books. The company was very small, in fact, and that meant a lot of work, and a lot of hassle. Small companies tend to be this way: you'll never have a shortage of work, and you tend to get responsibility thrown at you because there's no one else to do it. And things are more personal – for better and for worse!

Anyway, it wasn't long before I was handling more than just secretarial work, and, after a couple of months, I was offered a permanent position as a rights assistant, helping the MD on the administration of this side of the business. This meant a lot of direct communication with senior figures in publishing worldwide (for which a second or third language is indispensable), and something of a crash course in costings and profit calculations.

After two years in this position, I began to realise that the company was not likely to expand, and there was no room for me to develop myself any further. And so I secured a position with a major company almost on the doorstep of my home town, as an assistant rights manager in the Children's Division. The primary difference this made to my working life was in being responsible for a budget, and in travelling to book fairs both in the UK and abroad, primarily Frankfurt and Bologna. Book fairs are not nearly as glamorous as they sound and are extremely hard work!

After a couple of years, I began to get itchy feet again, and the introduction of very harsh financial stringencies in the company clinched it. On this occasion, I took my time to figure out the possibilities, as I wanted a responsible, long-term position. Patience and caution were rewarded in the end, as, after about five months, I was offered a job as Rights Manager with a fast-moving packager/publisher. I now spend about eight weeks a year on business trips abroad: Germany, Holland, Belgium, Scandinavia, Canada and the US are my main destinations. Once again, not really glamorous! I am kept on my feet with appointments to discuss the buying and selling of rights to books, along with costs, print runs, co-editions and freighting to consider. It's exhausting work and you've really got to put your soul into it. The satisfaction is in your increasing contacts, abilities, and experience, which all help to give you a measure of independence.

Copyright and Permissions Editor

In a company with a long backlist, this is a full-time job, and involves dealing with requests from individuals and other publishers to reproduce passages or illustrations from its copyright works. A good knowledge of the company's list is essential, as well as a knowledge of the publishing history of copyright titles. A good memory saves a lot of looking up. The implications of requests to reproduce may be far reaching, and the editor must be aware of them; if permission is granted (*always* in writing, never verbally), he decides whether a fee is to be charged, and, if so, how much.

It is a condition of most publishing contracts that the publisher will do his utmost to protect the copyright of author, illustrator or other publisher and, in common with all publishing staff, the copyright editor should be vigilant for cases of unlicensed reproduction. Illegal copying covers a wide field: photocopying and tape recording, often by educational establishments, plagiarism, and wholesale reproduction and sale of entire volumes of books by pirate companies the world over. Videos and cassettes are also prey to illegal copying; in fact, illegal copying covers anything where the originals are the property of others.

Companies can draw a substantial income from permissions, and even more so if they hold a large picture archive. They may have unofficial reciprocal arrangements; a publisher will be generous to those who are generous in return. Quotations used for review or criticism are the subject of general agreement, with fairly specific wordages allowed free. In some companies, the copyright responsibility will extend to obtaining permissions as well as granting them. Again, it is a job learned in the house and, as a rule, attached to the editorial department. A good standard of general education will be necessary, together with a knowledge of copyright – but this is usually acquired on the job.

Salary and Prospects
Salaries are commensurate with those in the editorial department. A copyright editor is unique and probably the only way to move is into another job in the same house or a similar job in

another company. If, however, one has a legal background, there may be scope for promotion as an adviser.

Royalties Clerk

The royalties clerk has accountancy training and has usually worked in the accounts department of a publishing house. The job entails a need to understand the terms in publishing contracts as they relate to payments due to authors and other publishers. Much of the recording work is held on computer, removing the former drudgery of keeping manual records.

The royalties clerk receives notification of all sales, and credits the relevant account with the sum due. In addition to royalties, the author is due a fixed percentage (spelt out in the contract) on advances and other payments received for subsidiary rights (paperback, book club, serialisation, radio, television, translation, and so on). The publisher pays out the sums accrued on the date stipulated in the contract - usually once a year (30 June), or twice a year (31 December as well) - to cover payments received in the royalty period ending three months before the payment date. Payment time is a period of intense activity for the royalties clerk who has to get all the accounts agreed on time and cheques prepared ready for simultaneous despatch. In large companies, this means hundreds of accounts to be agreed, and there are inevitable problems with returns for credit, accounts unpaid, and tax deductions for overseas authors. He needs to be knowledgeable about VAT, international and double taxation agreements, and able to settle the inevitable queries that roll in as soon as authors have checked their statements. The status of the royalties clerk depends greatly on his knowledge and expertise, and the best among them are valued advisers to both authors and publishers.

Chapter 3
Allied Occupations and Freelance Opportunities

Introduction

Literary agents have made themselves virtually indispensable since A P Watt founded the first one in London in 1875; the company continues today with a clientele of distinguished writers. Equally important to publishers is the swarming hive of small companies and freelance workers who provide editorial, literary, promotion, design and production services. The majority of those who offer these ancillary services were trained originally in publishing houses and have used initiative and entrepreneurial skills to set up on their own. This publishing fringe is itself a great source of freelance work, and calls on photographers, artists, cartographers, translators and typesetters for one-off jobs, mostly arising from personal publishing contacts and recommendations.

Literary Agents and Scouts

Literary agents are employed by many authors, who pay them about 10 per cent of receipts from home sales and up to 20 per cent on other sales for their services. The agent finds publishers for the author's works, and negotiates the best possible terms for his client. He deals with the publisher on all matters that affect his client, including the contract, manuscript delivery, follow-up titles, advertising and publicity, and obtaining payments when due. The agent frees the writer from time-consuming business matters which he may well be unqualified or unavailable to deal with.

Agents are usually responsible for the sale of non-print media rights in the text, an area in which few publishers are competent to work effectively. They may build up an expertise in the sale of film, radio, video, television or mechanical reproduction rights themselves, or have arrangements with other agents devoted exclusively to them, both here and abroad, but especially in the US.

Authors' agents may be consulted by publishers when they have a project in mind, but no writer. Agents frequently fulfil a creative role, reading manuscripts (for which some charge a fee) and making recommendations about them, even nursemaiding their clients at times, suggesting themes and subjects for their authors, evaluating their texts and possibly suggesting changes before submission to publishers. In this capacity they extend the editorial role, and many agents began, in fact, as editors. Some agents become personal friends of their authors, and are very supportive while they struggle with personal, financial and creative problems. Agents do not automatically accept as clients the authors who approach them. There is a limit to the number of authors to whom they can give a satisfactory service, and they look for evidence of literary ability coupled with sales potential before committing themselves to look after the author's interests.

Agents who act exclusively for publishers are known as *scouts*. They work in defined territories, actively seeking new authors, manuscripts and news of books being published abroad. The agent and scout role can be combined in one person - agenting for authors and scouting for a publisher at the same time; the interests may overlap but they may also conflict.

Scouts need wide contacts in the international publishing field, and must keep well informed. They are often commissioned by film and television companies to look out for books which would transfer satisfactorily to the screen; at the same time they protect the interests of their publishing clients by watching out for infringements of rights in their particular territories.

The largest agencies have several partners or directors and work in association with overseas agents, but the small establishment is more common - a few agents in partnership with a minimum of office support. There will rarely be recruitment into an agency, except at secretarial or personal assistant level - a level from which many have worked their way up. The rare vacancy will be filled by a publishing contact, headhunting or nepotism. Continuity of service is essential to avoid unsettling the clients. New agencies are founded annually - often by publishing rights managers deciding they have enough potential clients and contacts to go it alone.

Agents need shrewd literary judgement and a knowledge of

worldwide market conditions. Negotiating and legal skills, business ability and good money management are essential. They have to be hardworking, persistent and adaptable, with a sympathetic personality. Ther is no formal training; most have learned the job from working in a publishing house, and they continue learning by doing the job. Foreign languages are an asset, and essential in the international field.

Literary agents are listed in *The Writers' and Artists' Yearbook*, published annually by A & C Black. The members of the Association of Authors' Agents observe a code of professional practice and represent their clients' interests to the Publishers Association.

Publicists and Marketers

Independent publicists/marketers will have worked in publishing, journalism, advertising or public relations. They undertake a wide range of activities for a publisher on a freelance basis, from a single promotion to a complete publicity campaign. They may design, plan and print leaflets and catalogues, organise advertising, direct mailings, review copy distribution and press cuttings, arrange author tours, presentations and interviews and some will undertake print buying, sales and marketing.

Publicists are often individual freelances. The companies are usually small, and everyone must be able to tackle anything with aplomb. Here again, the entry is likely to be by recommendation and personal connections.

Editorial, Literary and Production Services

Companies offering the entire range of publishing services on a freelance basis sprang up in the 1979-82 recession, founded by publishing refugees, and their number has increased in the last decade. They recruit from experienced publishers, by recommendation, and offer a service to publishers, advertisers and public relations departments who need material to be written, prepared for press, researched, revised or updated, or pictures and maps provided. Many produce and manufacture discs, tapes, cassettes, slides and video films, which are often in demand for teaching and training.

Indexers

Publishers' contracts usually call on the author either to provide his own index, or to pay the cost of one provided by the publisher. Indexers tend to gain their initial experience in an editorial department by checking incoming indexes and preparing them for the printer. They are often prepared in great haste from paged galleys or page proofs, and may need tailoring to fit the pages available (the difference between the extent of the printed text and the nearest 'working' number of pages). A book is printed in multiples of 16 or 32 pages, so a text of 218 pages will have six pages for index, giving 224 pages in all. With learned works, encyclopaedias, journals and so on, an entire volume may be devoted to the index.

The indexer provides an alphabetical list of items in the book, together with the page numbers on which they appear; the items are listed at the publisher's behest, and the simplest index will consist of names of people and places only. In the past, this information was first entered on cards by hand and eventually the cards were typed up as lists on A4 sheets. Most indexers will now work directly on a personal computer and produce a disc for each index. Specialists will build up a personal reference library. Once an indexer builds up a connection with publishers, he will be booked in advance and given production dates, enabling him to plan his programme.

Training and Salary

While there is no formal training, the Society of Indexers offers a correspondence course. It gives a sound and comprehensive introduction to the principles and techniques of indexing. Practical supervision by a registered indexer is available to successful students who become members of the Society, and to other members who, without taking the course, have reached an equivalent level of competence. Details are given on page 73 and the course is likely to take from six to nine months. For detailed indexing of highly specialised works, subject knowledge is essential. The work requires meticulous application and patience so all indexers must possess these attributes. The indexer provides the last safety net for catching errors and inconsistencies in a work.

As most indexers work on a freelance basis there is no specific salary, but payment may be by the hour (the Society of Indexers asks £10.50 an hour for those on its register: 1994 rate), or a lump sum may be offered. (NUJ rate £11.75.) Alternatively, the indexer may be asked for a quotation after sight of the material.

The Society of Indexers
The Society aims to safeguard and improve indexing standards and to promote the professional interests of indexers. It issues an annual Register of Indexers who have satisfied the Society as to their practical ability in the compilation of indexes to books, periodicals and other publications, and this register is sent to all publishers. Membership confers no professional qualification. It ensures, however, that registered indexers are brought to the attention of all publishers who commission indexes.

Translators

Linguists have many careers open to them, of which translating is but one. It is usual to translate *into* one's mother tongue, and translators must be proficient writers. Fiction, in particular, requires considerable literary skill; the translator is, in effect, creating a new work, and it is through his mind that one nation is interpreted to another. In the non-fiction field, it is important to concentrate on subjects with which one is conversant, because of the technical and terminological knowledge required.

Translations are commissioned by publishers rather than authors, and it is necessary to establish yourself before being entrusted with a commission. Recommendation is invaluable, but if you have no connections it is worth approaching publishers directly, enclosing an abbreviated curriculum vitae with details of any translation or interpreting undertaken and, if possible, including a specimen of your work. Choose the international houses (Swiss, German and French houses who publish fairly specialised subjects) and UK publishers who buy in foreign originals and undertake their own translation; you will need to research this information. References may be asked for and, if you land a commission, it may be conditional upon prior approval of a lengthy extract from the book, so you must be prepared for this preliminary work. A translation is a heavy investment for a publishing house so it is reasonable to expect a monitoring of the result. A typewriter or word processor is essential. Increasingly, text is delivered on disc.

Translators are usually paid per 1000 words, starting at about £40 (NUJ rates from £84.40). Publishers prefer to pay an outright fee which includes copyright, but sometimes a royalty can be negotiated on reprints. See also below on readers' reports. The Translators Association offers its members legal and general advice. The annual subscription includes membership of the Society of Authors.

Freelance Opportunities

All freelance work is unreliable: at times there is no work at all; at others there is so much work that some has to be turned away. Payment for it may be irregular: some houses pay within a month; others take six. This is not a situation conducive to serenity when payment of your telephone bill depends on it; lack of a phone cuts you off from further work. Freelance workers are self-employed, with all the problems that implies: National Insurance contributions and benefits differ from those applying to employees and it is wise to invest in private health insurance and a pension scheme. The work is carried out under great pressure to close deadlines; a reputation for being an unreliable deliverer reduces the amount of work offered.

Freelance work offers opportunities for the housebound, but they are limited outside the London area or areas far from a nucleus of publishing activity. It is not for the inexperienced; in fact, a greater degree of expertise is called for as you are working alone and constantly need to make judgements and decisions. Most freelance work is obtained by personal recommendation, so a publishing background is essential. Also, many publishers prefer people who have worked in the business and know how books are produced, marketed and sold. Certain jobs have traditionally been placed outside the publishing house: indexing and translation, for example. Picture research is more often than not undertaken on a freelance basis.

Editorial

Expert readers' reports are commissioned, by the editorial department, on manuscripts or proposals which are being considered for publication. The reader is expected to have publishing knowledge, or be a specialist in the subject of the work, and know of rival publications which may affect the book's chances of success. He is usually chosen on the basis of existing contact or outside recommendation. Payment depends on the length and complexity of the task, but the minimum is likely to be £50 for a quick read through the text. A larger fee is common when specialist comment is called for, but it is usually a matter of personal negotiation depending on circumstances. If the reader is a specialist in great demand, or if the manuscript is very long, three figure fees are often charged. Similar terms are applicable to translators who are commissioned to prepare reports on foreign language texts being considered by a publisher.

The rewriting of manuscripts is often placed with freelance editors. The work ranges from anglicising an American text to revising heavily and polishing an inadequate translation, or a manuscript which has been written by a well-known 'name' whose writing ability does not equal his sales potential. Payment is either by an agreed fee for the whole job, or by a rate per 1000 words.

Copy editing and proof-reading are often farmed out to freelances on an hourly or piecework basis. They may undertake entire responsibility for a book, from copy editing through to camera-ready stage, for a fixed fee. This enables the freelance to subcontract. Payment starts at around £8 an hour, rising to £20+ depending on competence, expert knowledge and market forces.

Typesetting
With the advent of the personal computer, straight manuscript typing is increasingly done by authors. However, it may still be commissioned by the author or publisher. The keyboard operator will often copy edit, imposing house style on the text, and typeset straight to page. It is wise to examine the material before agreeing to a rate per page or for the entire job.

Lexicography
This is the preparation of definitions which appear in dictionaries and other reference books. Lexicographers usually start in-house, on the compilation of a dictionary under the direction of an editor, and then become freelances. Specialist subject knowledge or a degree may be required, but a talent for words is paramount. A large proportion of lexicography is carried out on a freelance basis, commissioned by the major dictionary and reference work publishers. As the English language is perpetually changing, updating the files is a constant occupation.

Reference Books
Encyclopaedia and yearbook entries are usually compiled by freelance writers with specialist knowledge. The work is commissioned by publishers, usually on a recommendation basis. Payment is either per entry or per 1000 words.

Design and Illustration
Most illustrations are produced by freelance artists; there is a constant demand for cover and jacket designs and layouts, as well as for the design of all printed matter used by publishing houses, design companies, advertising firms, and companies wanting their own promotional material and letterheads. Much of this will be carried out on a desk-top publishing system.

Sales Representatives
Freelance sales reps may travel for several publishers in a designated area; a few small lists can be combined into a worthwhile group, something that the small publishers could not achieve by themselves. They will contribute proportionally to the sales rep's commission and expenses.

Picture Research
Picture researchers usually start their professional lives in photographic agencies, galleries, museums or publishing houses. Once established, they have the choice of either working for a company or turning freelance. When they freelance for a publisher, an engagement form for each assignment specifies the researcher's exact responsibilities; her reputation will be at stake if the publisher fails to carry out his part of the work which involves the prompt return of borrowed material and prompt payment of all fees. Payment is commonly a fee per book or per picture.

A picture researcher may move into the photographic field, starting as a props girl (providing properties for photographic settings) and then becoming a stylist (conceiving and commissioning every aspect of photographic shots, with responsibility for engaging photographers, models, hiring props and paying fees) for world-renowned glossy magazines and partworks and the best women's magazines. Such commissions pay around £80 to £240 a day. Experience as a stylist can lead to the art editorship of a top magazine. Business acumen is essential, the ability to handle people, as well as all the qualities and expertise of a picture researcher.

Opportunities outside publishing lie within television, video, audio-visual productions, design companies, exhibition design and advertising. Work in television can start with research, but may include rostrum work (directing the cameraman on the important focusing areas of a still picture). Membership of the Broadcasting Entertainment Cinematograph Theatre Union

(BECTU) is essential for television researchers after the probationary period.

Case Study

Jessica is a Freelance Editor and works from home.

> I went straight into the industry after completing my English degree. My first job was with a company providing bibliographic services, working on the book information itself. Not very exciting, but steady work, and it made a good introduction to the publishing world. I was put in charge of the section after about a year. It was a good company, and was making the change from being rather old fashioned. I also got involved with some publishing societies while there and started to make lots of contacts.
>
> After three years, I felt like a change, and had already undertaken some extra-curricular courses in editing skills and DTP. I was taken on as an editor in the publishing arm of a major media company, working mainly on business textbooks and guides. It was very good experience, but I didn't really like the pressure, which was immense, and the impersonality of a large organisation.
>
> I moved on to a smaller company which specialised in business training, and produced a good line of associated textbooks. These were very happy days, being responsible for your own work, and taking projects from author to warehouse. And I felt an affinity with the approach of the company, which was very liberal. Perhaps that is why they started running into difficulties. Whatever the case, I felt I could see the writing on the wall, and I wondered what to do.
>
> I don't know when exactly I made the decision, but I made up my mind to go freelance. The main thing about this is that you need contacts, above all else. These I had, and I was able to start up almost immediately as a proof-reader, with a borrowed PC and a dining table in my bedroom! Since then, business has boomed, and I now do research and editing as well.
>
> Having said that, you earn a living from such work, but you won't get rich. And you work long hours. The prime requisite is attention to detail and a common-sense, logical approach. After that, speed of work, and reliability. The obstacles are in getting work when you need it, rather than all at once, and in getting paid. And you really have to dedicate yourself to your books. Remember at all times that you are a business. The taxman does!

Chapter 4
Booksellling

Introduction

Books are sold in many kinds of shops where product knowledge is not required – such as newsagents, bargain outlets, supermarkets, DIY warehouses and garden centres, to name but a few – as well as the book departments of large stores, including W H Smith. Here we discuss shops selling new stock bought from publishers and wholesalers.

Sales depend heavily on dedicated book buyers, impulse buyers, attractive window displays, special promotions, publishers' advertising, review coverage in print and broadcast media, and word-of-mouth recommendation. Shops with sufficient resources strive to open institutional accounts with local businesses and libraries. Mail order sales to customers abroad can be built up over time, but this activity is mainly confined to shops in London and university catchment areas.

Bookselling tends to be a young profession with a fair amount of staff turnover, leaving the stayers to move up into management. People leave for a variety of reasons: to do something completely different or to go into publishing, where the bookshop experience is valuable. The shops obviously look to recruit those who will stay and be trained up, not move on. However, there are good and bad employers, and some try to employ all staff on a temporary basis, offering no paid holidays, so that no employment rights are acquired. It is important to find out what the current situation is if you are seeking a career.

People who love books but are undecided about what they want to do with their lives often make bookselling their first choice of career. It is an enjoyable job which offers a reasonable living, but not a good one.

The Booksellers' Association of Great Britain and Northern Ireland (BA) is the trade organisation. It represents members' interests to the publishing trade, Parliament and the general public. Its annual conference provides a meeting place and forum for discussion. The BA also develops and administers training courses, leading to the Certificate in Bookselling Skills.

Publishers exhibit at the annual conference, as well as at the London International Book Fair, held at Olympia in spring. Booksellers at both events have the opportunity to see a mass of new books and discuss their accounts.

Working in a Bookshop

Except in business bookshops, which tend to keep office hours, it may be necessary to work long hours, including weekends, bank holidays and late evenings. These are usually balanced out by a flexible working arrangement and the use of part-time and temporary staff at busy times. These contingent workers are well placed to slip into permanent jobs when they become vacant.

The normal range of tasks involved in retailing applies: buying, selling, dealing with customers' enquiries, unpacking, checking stock, stock-taking, keeping shelves filled, tidy and dusted, window display, packing and despatching orders and returns, handling cash and making payments, and some pricing. As most books already bear a net price, less ticketing is involved than in other retailers. (The Net Book Agreement permits price reductions only in well-defined circumstances.) Special promotions and author signing sessions are co-ordinated with publishers.

Customer relations are of vital importance; customers build up a rapport with their favourite shops and a never-ending supply of new titles can induce them to spend heavily. Their enquiries can be difficult to handle: straightforward enough when the customer has full details of the book sought, by bringing in a review, for example, but less so when the request is for something less easily traced: 'There's a girl's face on the front cover – it's called Love something or Something love'!

Detailed product knowledge is essential, as well as keeping informed of current trends and knowing what has been reviewed. Large stores will have specialists in charge of the subject sections (fiction, history, travel, music, education, and so on) who can be paged to deal with specific enquiries. The range of product knowledge called for is the main difference between bookselling and other forms of retailing, as well as the need to match books to the right customers when consulted.

Sales staff need to be enthusiastic sellers – the purpose of their job. Despite the reputation bookshops have of being havens for browsers, sales must be made for them to stay in business.

The work involves standing all day, not sitting. Back pain is a hazard of the job – books are heavy and staff are taught how to handle parcels correctly. But comfort can be improved by a well-designed shop, which makes deliveries easier to bring in. Jobs are rotated among staff, so they take turns at checking goods inwards against orders and invoices, and arranging them on the stacks.

In a small shop, buying will be done by the manager; in larger shops, section heads or department heads do the buying. They will examine publishers' advance information, study their lists and see visiting sales representatives, place orders for forthcoming books and restock with backlist titles.

In some groups, W H Smith for example, there is a high degree of central buying of new titles, with stocks being scaled out according to branch size and importance. Individual shops can, of course, order in titles that will sell well in their area.

Shop managers may well have an expenditure budget; if purchases are in danger of overrunning it, allocations to subject sections will be reduced. In such situations, best sellers naturally benefit, as they ensure that profits will be maintained.

The lack of opportunity to buy can be frustrating for assistants in small shops. It is important for career development to get buying experience.

Education and Training

There are no specific entry requirements, but a good general education is essential. Most entrants are graduates, often with a degree in English. It is important to match your subject interest to a bookshop which offers that subject, be it fiction, science, medicine, mountaineering, religion or natural history.

Training starts on the job; for product knowledge, procedures and systems, an in-house session will be held at fixed times before the shop opens. Training courses are described in Chapter 5.

Salary and Prospects

All retailers suffered during the recession, with bookshops no exception. The result is that staffing has been pared to a minimum, and many salaries pegged or even reduced. Starting salaries are very low, from £6,000 to £7,000 a year for sales assistants; up to £8,500 for senior assistants. Higher rates are paid in London. The trade is cagey on the subject and exact figures are hard to come by. Figures quoted in advertisements tend to be for experienced staff only; managers of large shops can earn upwards of £20,000.

Prospects for promotion are good once experience has been gained, provided the business is sound.

Applying for Jobs

Although there are over 3,000 bookshop members of the BA, listed in the BA directory, jobs are more likely to be available in the big retail chains (which may include university bookshops and shops within libraries and department stores). The many small independent shops tend to be owner managed, and have fewer staff.

It is always worth applying on spec to branches of large groups, where the manager will engage the staff. Lower-level jobs are rarely advertised, so use all the contacts you have and keep an eye on the classified advertisements in the *Bookseller*, which will probably be available at the desk of public libraries or their reference section. Advertisements in the past year (1993-94) included:

- School/college leaver required for stock room and packing duties.
- Part-time assistant bookseller required to work 11am to 3pm five days a week.
- Full-time bookseller required with at least nine months' experience to make a career with us; Saturdays and extended hours necessary on a rota basis.
- Retail manager required for a university bookshop, with responsibility for two others in the same county, and a total staff complement of 43. The manager would be responsible for all aspects of the business including retail sales, library supply, finance, marketing, administration, EPOS (electronic point of sale) and all the support functions essential to maintain a business of this size. The benefits package includes a performance-related bonus, company car, contributory pension and assistance with relocation; salary £20,000-£23,000.

Part 2

Chapter 5
Training in Publishing and Bookselling

PUBLISHING

Introduction

For many graduates, including graduates of specialist publishing courses, finding a job is very difficult indeed. Even so, it is surprising how many people apply for jobs in publishing with no knowledge of the industry at all, and with no relevant skills other than a vague love of books. Your chances can be improved considerably with a little effort.

- Get informed - read the *Bookseller* and *Publishing News*, the trade weeklies which are available at the desk of most public libraries. Read the media pages and the book reviews of the national newspapers.
- If possible, get a holiday or Saturday job in a bookshop - packing, unpacking, ordering, checking, selling - anything. You will learn about what happens to a book after it leaves the publisher, which publishers have efficient distribution, accounting and representation. Alternatively, library work, or retail or office work of any kind is always useful. If you can't get a job, volunteer to help out in return for the valuable experience.
- Browse in a range of bookshops. How are the books presented? What are people buying? Why? What attracts people into the shop to start with? Observe signing sessions and in-store promotions. Which books are in the bargain basement stores?
- Visit other book retail outlets such as supermarkets, large stores, DIY shops, newsagents, airports, railway stations and motorway service stations.
- Go to your local public library and look at the selection of books available. Study the organisation of the library itself, the cataloguing system, the reference books at the desk and the bibliographic reference system (whether computerised or on cards). Find out what is borrowed, and why.

- Visit book fairs, printing exhibitions and literary festivals. The main UK book trade event is the London International Book Fair held at Olympia every spring.
- Attend any public lectures you can – look at the programmes issued by your local education authority, the extra-mural department of your nearest university, and the local Workers' Educational Association.
- Look at all the marketing bumph you receive through the post, particularly from book clubs, and compare different techniques. Look at how it works. What is it trying to do? Does it succeed?
- Send for the seasonal catalogues of several publishers. What imprints do they have? Are the lists linked? How is the information set out?
- Watch book and publishing programmes on television and listen to literary programmes on the radio.
- Last, but certainly not least, *read*. It goes without saying that to be considering a career in publishing, particularly on the editorial side, you must be passionate about books.

Publishing is a rare industry in that experience of a variety of areas within publishing, or related areas such as bookselling or librarianship, is considered valuable. No department can work in isolation and an awareness of wider issues is useful. Many people start in small companies where they can 'learn the ropes' of everything from customer service to marketing through design and estimating, before moving on to a more specialised position in a larger company. Such an overview is also essential for a successful publishing start-up.

Publishing companies are notorious for the lack of formal training opportunities, and often rely on 'learn-as-you-go' training, usually supplied by a more experienced colleague, particularly for editorial skills. This works well, but the cost to the company is concealed. However, cost-conscious publishers need employees who can begin to contribute to company profit as quickly as possible, without requiring a long learning curve, so previous related experience, even by means of informal study, is desirable.

A far wider range of training options for publishers has become available in recent years. In particular, the advent of desk-top publishing has led to a multitude of new short courses which include the production of newsletters and promotional catalogues. An example is the range of courses set up recently by

Middlesex University Small Press Centre, aimed at self-publishers. (See below for details.) Gloucestershire College of Art and Technology is currently trialling courses for publishing in pre-press, print procedures and media technology.

Specific Careers

Training for designers, which is essential for employment in publishing, is described fully in *Careers in Art and Design* (Kogan Page, 1992). Designers who plan to enter publishing should choose a course with a strong typographical content to enable them to work on page make-up, jacket design, promotional materials, and so on. Computer design skills, such as desktop publishing ability, are very useful.

Printing is a highly organised trade which offers its own careers to skilled operatives, but some skills are transferable to publishing. The British Printing Industries Federation can provide full details of training, qualifications and careers (see Useful Addresses, Chapter 8).

Degree and Postgraduate Diploma Courses

Many of the new universities now offer a publishing option in their degree courses, taking the lead from the well-established modular degree course at Oxford Brookes University (formerly Oxford Polytechnic).

The other well-established course, though less well known within the publishing industry, is the BA (Hons) Publishing at Napier University (formerly Napier Polytechnic), which has recently achieved degree status. A list follows:

University of Brighton
MA/Postgraduate Diploma Fine Art (Printmaking)
MA/Postgraduate Diploma Fine Art (Narrative Illustration and Editorial Design)

Falmouth School of Art and Design
BA (Hons) Graphic Information Design (4 yrs sandwich)
BA (Hons) Visual Communication (3 yrs FT)

Leeds University
MA Bibliography, Publishing and Textual Studies

London College of Printing and Distributive Trades
BA (Hons) Book Production (5 yrs PT)
BA (Hons) Publishing (4 yrs PT) – subject to validation

66 *Careers in Publishing and Bookselling*

Postgraduate Diploma in Printing and Publishing Studies (17 wks FT)

Loughborough University
BA (Hons) Information and Publishing (3 yrs FT/4 yrs sandwich)

Middlesex University
BA Writing and Publishing with another subject (3 yrs FT)
MA Computer Integrated Publishing (1 yr FT)

Napier University, Edinburgh
BA/BA (Hons) Publishing (3/4 yrs FT)

Nottingham Trent University
BA (Hons) Print Media Management (HND course plus 1 yr FT)

Oxford Brookes University
BA/BSc (Joint Hons) Publishing and another subject (3 yrs FT)
BA/BSc/BEd/LLB/DipHE/Certificate modular qualifications in a range of subjects with Publishing modules
Postgraduate Diploma Advanced Studies in Publishing (1 yr FT)

University of Plymouth
Postgraduate Diploma Publishing and Book Production (30 wks FT)
MA Publishing and Book Production (30 wks FT plus 15 wks FT/1 yr PT)

Reading University
BA (Hons) Typography and Graphic Communication (4 yrs FT)
Postgraduate Diploma Typography and Graphic Communication (1 yr FT)
PhD/MPhil Typography and Graphic Communication

Robert Gordon University, Aberdeen
BA/BA (Hons) Publishing Studies (3/4 yrs FT)

University of Stirling
MPhil/Postgraduate Diploma Publishing Studies (1 yr FT)

Swansea Institute of Higher Education
BA (Hons) Art and Media Studies (Publishing and Print) (3 yrs FT; PT available)

Thames Valley University
BA (Hons) Information Management (Publishing and Information Studies) (3 yrs FT)
Postgraduate Diploma Information Management (Publishing) (1 yr FT/ 2 yrs PT)
MA Information Management (Publishing) (1 yr FT/2 yrs PT)

West Herts College, Watford
BSc (Hons) Graphic Media Studies (Publishing with Printing or Business Management or Printing and Packaging Technology) (4 yrs sandwich)

Postgraduate Diploma Publishing (25 wks FT)
Postgraduate Diploma Creative Writing and Promotional Copywriting (25 wks FT)

Wolverhampton University
BA (Hons) Electronic Media (Design for Print) with one or two other subjects (3 yrs FT; PT available)

BTEC/SCOTVEC Courses

Aberdeen College
SCOTVEC HNC/HND Graphic Design

Cardonald College, Glasgow
SCOTVEC HNC Graphic Design

Clackmannan College, Alloa
SCOTVEC HNC Graphics and Illustration

Dumfries and Galloway College
SCOTVEC HNC Graphics and Illustration

Dundee College
SCOTVEC HNC/HND Graphic Design

Falkirk College
SCOTVEC HNC/HND Graphic Design

Falmouth School of Art and Design
BTEC HND Copywriting and Art Direction (2 yrs FT)
BTEC HND Graphic Design (Typographic Design or Design for Print) (2 yrs FT)
BTEC ND Graphic Design (Typographic Design or Design for Print) (2 yrs FT)

Glasgow College of Building and Printing
SCOTVEC Advanced Diploma in Medical Illustration
SCOTVEC HNC/HND Design for Printing
SCOTVEC HNC Electronic Publishing
SCOTVEC HNC Graphic Reproduction
SCOTVEC HND Information and Media Technology with Visual Communications
SCOTVEC HNC Printing Management and Production
SCOTVEC HNC/HND Technical Graphics

Gloucestershire College of Arts and Technology, Gloucester
BTEC HND Media: Publishing and Information Management (2 yrs FT)

London College of Printing and Distributive Trades
BTEC ND Graphic and Typographic Design (2 yrs FT)

BTEC ND Business and Finance with Introduction to Publishing option (2 yrs FT)
BTEC HND Typographic Design (2 yrs FT)
BTEC HND Business and Finance (Publishing Management) (2 yrs FT)
BTEC HND Design (Bookbinding) (2 yrs FT)
Diploma Publishing Production (35 wks FT)

Nene College, Northampton
BTEC HND Design (Print Media Management) (2 yrs FT)

Nottingham Trent University
BTEC HND Print Media Management (3 yrs sandwich)

Telford College, Edinburgh
SCOTVEC HNC Design and Typography for Print (2 yrs PT)
SCOTVEC HND Design and Typography for Print (2 yrs FT)
SCOTVEC HNC Illustration and Media Design (2 yrs PT)
SCOTVEC HND Illustration and Media Design (2 yrs FT)

West Herts College, Watford
BTEC ND/HND Typographic Design (2 yrs FT)
BTEC HND Printing, Publishing and Packaging (2 yrs FT/3 yrs sandwich)

Wolverhampton University
BTEC HND Design (Electronic Design for Print) (2 yrs FT)

National Vocational Qualifications

The Publishing Qualifications Board (PQB) administers National Vocational Qualifications (NVQs) for the publishing industry. In 1994 the PQB joined forces with the Open University Validation Services (OUVS) to promote NVQs. From 1995, publishing NVQs should also be available via the Open University.

NVQs are currently available in eight subjects: Book Editing (Levels 3 and 4); Editorial Management; Commissioning; Book Production; Book Design; Publicity; Book Publishing Rights; and Book Publishing Contracts. Pilots are taking place currently (early 1994) on two courses: Journal Management and Programme Development (Level 4); and Journal Production Editing (Level 4). Copies of the NVQ scheme books and guidance notes are available at £5 each (see Useful Addresses, Chapter 8).

NVQs are assessed in the workplace by trained assessors with relevant expertise, although it is also possible for freelances to take NVQs. Candidates must demonstrate competence in areas of work called *units*. Each unit is divided into *elements of competence*, and each element is accompanied by a number of *performance criteria* whose breadth is specified in the *range statement*. *Evidence required*, of both performance and knowledge, is also specified.

There are no entry requirements, but 18 months' experience is recommended. Candidate registration is £175 plus VAT (Level 3) and £200 plus VAT (Level 4) (1993).

Short Courses

Book House Training Centre
This registered charity operates as a self-financing body, providing over 100 training courses each year to employees in the publishing industry. Tutors are publishing professionals, in house, consultants or freelances, and often have a training or teaching background.

BHTC offers courses of one to five days' duration, some of which are residential, on all aspects of publishing at every level, from entry to senior management. Prices range from £75 plus VAT to £1,250 plus VAT; the courses are intensive and most delegates are sponsored by their companies. Although the majority of courses are intended to be in-service vocational training, a few may be of interest to people thinking of going into publishing.

The courses available in 1994 are divided into the following broad subject areas: foundation training, editorial training, publishing and the law, production training, computers in publishing, marketing training, distribution, publishing finance, and management training.

In addition, BHTC runs two evening classes, each with eight two-hour sessions: Copy-editing Skills and Picture Research. Both are priced £285 plus VAT (1994).

For anyone wanting to study completely independently, BHTC publishes *Basic Editing: A Practical Course*, two volumes (a textbook and an exercise book) by Nicola Harris. Priced at £27.50 (plus £2.50 postage and packing), it is addressed to those wishing to make a career in book or journal publishing (see Chapter 8).

Gloucestershire College of Arts and Technology, Gloucester
Day and evening courses in desk-top publishing, lithographic printing and screen process printing are available. Evening

courses run for six sessions of two hours each (£60) and day courses last for six hours (£175 one-to-one tuition).

Oxford Brookes University
The University Short Course Unit offers four eight-week evening classes in publishing – Copy Editing: Core Skills: Proof-Reading: Core Skills; On-Screen Editing: Core Skills; and Book Design: An Introductory Course. They also present a one-day course entitled Computer Essentials for Editors.

London School of Publishing
The London School of Publishing runs a range of ten-week evening classes (all at £300 inc VAT): Editorial (Parts 1 and 2); Magazine Editorial; Production (Books); Art Production; Picture Research; Book Commissioning; Marketing and Promotion for Publishers; DTP (Quark XPress/PageMaker 5/Ventura Gold); Children's Books; Contracts and Rights. It also has branches in Oxford and New York.

London College of Printing and Distributive Trades
The LCPDT offers a range of more general short courses which run throughout the year, including How to Publish Yourself; Publishing as a Small Business Venture; Publishing as a Career Option; An Introduction to Publishing; Editorial Management; Publishing Management; and several desk-top publishing courses. These vary from one-day intensive courses to ten-week evening classes, and are organised by the Professional Development Unit of the London Institute.

Middlesex University
The Small Press Centre organises a series of evening classes for self-publishers. The six 13-week courses are priced at £129.25 inc VAT (1993/94) each. Topics are: Handprinting and the Small Press, Artists' Books, Producing Your Own Publication, Illustrating and Designing by Computer, Business and the Small Publisher, and Outsider Publishing – The Real Freedom of Presses.

Password Training
One- or two-day courses in London: Foundation Course in Publishing; Marketing for Publishers; Beginner's guide to Desk-top Publishing. Prices from £111 (inc VAT) to £229 (inc VAT) (1994). In-house and tailor-made courses are also available.

Grants are provided for small publishers by the Paul Hamlyn Foundation (see page 78).

Training Matters
An independent training and consultancy organisation, geared specifically for the publishing industry. Off-the-shelf or tailored in-house courses are available in the following areas: managing projects; team building; negotiating skills; appraisal training; influencing skills; introduction to publishing; time and self management; finance for non-financial staff; personal effectiveness/assertiveness, recruitment practice; telesales training.

They also offer consultancy and careers guidance services.

West Herts College, Watford
Day and evening, basic and advanced desk-top publishing courses, including City & Guilds 7261 Desk-top Publishing. One-day to one-week courses on book, magazine and journal production. BTEC Continuing Education Certificates by distance learning, including courses on publishing and creative writing and copywriting.

University of Westminster
The Short Course Unit provides several evening and one-day, weekend or five-day courses in desk-top publishing, sub-editing and writing, aimed primarily at journalists.

Courses Organised by Societies

Association of Learned and Professional Society Publishers
The ALPSP organises occasional seminars, often in association with other professional organisations such as the UK Serials Group, on a wide range of issues relevant to society publishers, such as Electronic Books and Multimedia, Publishing in the New World, Saving Money on Administration, Journal Design, Working with Printers, and Software for Small Publishers.

British Library Centre for the Book
The British Library set up the Centre for the Book to promote the significance of the book, from manuscript to final product, including the new media.

The Centre holds seminars on new technology in publishing. Subjects in early 1994 were Bookshops and Automation, Book Clubs and Bookshops in the Future (cost £15 each). A regular series of popular lectures covers all aspects of making a book, past and present. Conferences, often in association with other organisations, address topics that go beyond national boundaries, such as the nature and impact of Anglo-American publishing, the impact of the European Single Market, Third World publishing and censorship.

Institute of Scientific and Technical Communicators
The ISTC organises occasional one-day seminars on the basic principles of indexing books and journals, among other topics, priced £95 (£105 for non-members) (1994). Venues include London, Newcastle upon Tyne and Coventry.

Oxford Publicity Partnership
Founded in 1989 to provide a range of publicity services to academic, educational and professional publishers, it offers one- or two-day courses, mainly for people in marketing departments, on: Press and PR; Introduction to Journals Publishing; Introduction to Publicity; Copywriting; Printed Publicity for Direct Mail. One-day courses cost £150 plus VAT with two-day courses costing £250 plus VAT (1994). In-house training is possible for the Copywriting and the Introduction to Publicity courses.

Oxford Women in Publishing
Oxford Women in Publishing hold six meetings a year (£2 for non-members). The Society runs a number of one-day courses for women, held on Saturdays in central Oxford. The 1994 programme covers: Introduction to Desk-top Publishing; Moving into Commissioning; Finance Made Easy; Copy editing Level I (beginners); Copy editing Level II (improvers); Introduction to Publishing. These cost £35 (£40 non-members). Personal Effectiveness: Improving Managerial Performance is a two-day course, priced £56 (£70 non-members). A number of assisted places are available for each of these courses.

Society of Freelance Editors and Proofreaders
The Society is a non-profit-making organisation founded in 1988 to reflect the increasing importance of freelances to the industry. It aims both to promote high editorial standards and achieve recognition of the professional status of its members.

The SFEP is setting up an accreditation scheme for its

freelance members. The proposed scheme would consist of three classes of SFEP membership:

- Member: by paying annual subscription.
- Accredited member: by successful completion of SFEP test.
- Registered member: by (a) SFEP test, a minimum of two years' experience within three years and forms of approval from two client publishers; and (b) at least 2000 hours' experience within five years and approval forms from three publishers.

The Society offers a wide range of one-day workshop courses, for freelances or in-house staff, at venues around the country, notably in London and Edinburgh: Introduction to Proof-reading; Proof-reading Problems; Introduction to Copy editing; Brush up Your Copy editing; Efficient Copy editing; References; Introduction to Illustrations; Marking Up Manuscripts for Interfacing; Brush Up Your Grammar; Going Freelance and Staying There; Running a One-person Business; Personal Effectiveness. Prices range from £40 to £50 for members, £82.50 to £92.50 for non-members.

New one-day workshops planned for 1994 are a post-beginner copy-editing workshop based on Nicola Harris's *Basic Editing: A Practical Course* (BHTC; see page 69) and an introduction to on-screen editing.

The Whitcombe Training Fund was set up in 1993 with the aim of providing training for freelances and work experience through mentoring programmes.

Society of Indexers

The Society administers an open learning indexing course. This comprises five units, priced £10–£15 (£15–£20 for non-members) each. Further optional units are planned. Self-administered tests are available at £1. Formal test papers are available only to members, priced £12–£17 each, and tutorial support is possible at £9.75 per hour.

Occasional indexing training workshops are held at venues around the country for beginners/novices, for newly/nearly accredited indexers and for those more experienced. Specialist workshops are run on topics such as Computers in Indexing and Thesaurus Construction. The cost for these one-day workshops is £35 (£40 for non-members) (1994).

General techniques of indexing are usually included in the curriculum of Schools of Librarianship.

UK Serials Group
UKSG organises a programme of courses, seminars and workshops around the UK for librarians and publishers of serials and journals, for example, Series Administration and Management; The Journal at the Crossroads; Taming the Electronic Jungle.

Women in Publishing
WiP was founded in 1979 to promote the status of women working in publishing and related trades. One-day courses, open to all women, are taught by senior women from within and beyond the book trade, and are priced £45 (£65 for non-members).

The following topics are covered on the 1994 training programme: Introduction to book publishing; Principles of marketing; Basic book costings; Working freelance; Selling rights; the commissioning editor's role; Taking charge of your career; Management skills; The author/publisher contract; Editorial project management. There is also a weekend residential course on Developing your potential, priced £175 (£350 for non-members) which includes a follow-up day.

The Society holds monthly meetings at the Publishers Association, and has set up a mentoring network to support, advise and encourage women in developing their careers in publishing. It has produced a book, *Reviewing the Reviews: A Woman's Place on the Book Page* (1987, Journeyman).

Correspondence Courses

There are now a number of correspondence courses offering editorial training for the individual. Such courses are usually advertised in the *Guardian* and the *Bookseller*.

Freelance MS
This is an editorial correspondence course, costing £56.95 (plus VAT) (1994), with no previous experience required, for those wanting to work from home. The course comprises an introduction and information file, a short edited manuscript for reference, a set of proofs to work on, and a set of marked-up proofs for checking against. A self-assessment scorecard is also included. There is a free advisory service for one year after successful completion, and an advanced course, costing £52.50 (plus VAT), is also available.

Chapterhouse Publishing
Exeter-based Chapterhouse runs a range of courses, either by distance learning, six-week courses or intensive four-day courses: Editorial Skills; Editorial Skills Beginner; Proof-reader Express; Basic Editing; Better English.

National Extension College
The NEC has revived and updated its Editing for Everyone correspondence course. This six-assignment course, now called Essential Editing, is priced at £140 inc VAT (1994). The course is aimed at those new to editing and provides tutor-marked assignments on basic principles. Study topics include proof-reading, planning a publication and passing copy to print. A good standard of English, to at least GCSE grade C or equivalent, is required. The accompanying coursebook by Sally Vince and Celia Hall can be purchased separately at £34.95. The NEC is also planning a desk-top publishing correspondence course.

Rapid Results College
The new School for Writers features a Successful Copy Writing course costing £79 inc VAT (1993/94).

BOOKSELLING

Although smaller booksellers recognise the importance of training, the familiar 'Catch 22' excuse is perpetuated – there is no time or money for training even though, once trained, the bookseller may well be more efficient and generate more income.

Bookselling skills, as with many other retail industries, tend to to be learned on the job. Staff can, to a certain extent, train themselves by becoming familiar with the products and the trade publications, and by learning how to use sources of information such as reference books, publishers' catalogues, microfiches and computer databases.

Larger stores and chains, such as W H Smith, have complex staff induction and refresher training schemes covering all aspects of customer service, stock control and product knowledge. Many shops will assist staff wishing to acquire the Certificate in Bookselling Skills (CIBS) administered by BA Training (see below). A range of courses organised by BA Training is useful for staff at all levels. Unlike publishing, there are no HNC/D, degree or postgraduate-level courses in this area, and few other means of obtaining training on an individual basis.

Courses

BA Training

The Booksellers Association of Great Britain and Ireland promotes training to its members. Its training arm, BA Training, presents a full complement of training schemes for bookshop staff.

Certificate in Bookselling Skills

Successful completion of both levels of the nationally recognised bookselling qualification – Certificate in Bookselling Skills (CIBS) – is evidence that a bookseller has attained the standard of bookselling skills and knowledge needed up to senior assistant level. This carefully structured but flexible open-learning course is studied through a number of manuals. Students work mostly at home, at their own pace and mainly in their own time. The practical coursework is completed in the bookshop and the internal trainer will help with fitting this around other duties.

Level 1, covering basic bookselling and retailing skills needed for working on the shop floor, tackles such topics as dealing with customers, handling money, ensuring the security and safety of the shop and its occupants, dealing with stock and knowing how to use trade reference books. At this level, students are supervised by an experienced bookseller in the bookshop where they work. This level is ideal for staff in their first three months of bookshop work, and relates to the actual procedures and practices being used in your bookshop.

Level 2 goes into more factual detail and covers stock knowledge, book evaluation, marketing, shop layout and display, basic finance, staff supervision and so on. Written assignments are assigned by an external tutor who is also available for assistance and advice. Most of the exercises and work projects relate to the particular needs and circumstances of your own bookshop.

The first study pack, comprising Study Guide, Trainer's Guide, Induction Guide and Level 1 Manual, costs £65 (VAT not payable), and two Level 2 Manuals. The second study pack consists of two Level 1 Manuals and a Glossary of book trade terminology and costs £128.40 (inc VAT) (1994).

CIBS is open to anyone working in a bookshop. No previous experience or academic qualifications are required. The CIBS course can also be incorporated into existing staff-training programmes. A leaflet is available which lists more of the topics covered in the CIBS course.

National Vocational Qualifications
A series of National Vocational Qualifications (NVQs) for booksellers will be introduced by BA Training over the next few years. A new Foundation in Bookselling course, which is intended to underpin the NVQ studies, is being introduced during 1994. This will gradually replace the established CIBS course. Full details of this course and the NVQs are available from BA Training.

Short Courses
BA Training runs a comprehensive collection of courses of varied duration in the form of traditional training course, seminar and workshop. The training schedule for the first part of 1994 covers the following courses:

- *Half-day courses:* Shop Floor Security; Devising Staff Incentive Schemes.
- *One-day courses:* Using the Media; Assertiveness in the Workplace – Handling Difficult People and Situations; Introduction to Display and Merchandising Skills; Exploiting Financial Strengths and Eliminating the Weaknesses of Your Business; Surviving as an Independent; Introduction to Bookselling; Finance for Non-financial Managers; Children's Bookselling; The Booksellers' Marketing Mix; Introduction to Buying; Preparing the Business Plan; Exporting Documentation and VAT Implications; Mail Order.
- *Two-day course:* Successful Negotiation Techniques for Management.
- *Three-day residential course:* Management Skills for Booksellers.

Prices range from £49.50 for a half day to £599.00 for the three-day residential course.

Other short courses run regularly by BA Training include: Developing Specialised Markets; Customer Service Strategies; Key Legal Responsibilities for Booksellers (Part 1: Advertising and Trading Standards; Part 2: Employment Law, Data Protection, Health and Safety); Future Trends in UK Retailing; Introduction to Buying; How to Make Your Computer Earn its Keep.

Training Plans for Bookshops
BA Training also provides a unique series of ready-to-use in-

house staff training plans, entitled 'A Vital 30 Minutes', which are ideal for use at the start or finish of the working day. Covering every aspect of bookselling, the 52 half-hour training plans are practical and easy to use. They can be customised for individual bookshops if necessary. A free sample is available.

Other Training Providers

Andrea Marks PR
Tailor-made full- or half-day courses for individuals, designed for bookshop owners and managers.

Book House Training Centre
BHTC has published a book jointly with UNESCO entitled *Successful Bookselling: A Management Training Course* (price £29.99). Topics covered include a survey of the book trade, sites and premises, shop layout, customer contact skills, finance and budgeting, time planning and administration, book-buying, principles of stock control and bibliographic services.

Frances Lincoln
This London-based publishing company have developed a mutually beneficial exchange scheme with booksellers.

Funding for Training

Paul Hamlyn Foundation
The Paul Hamlyn Foundation supports training and education for publishing and bookselling. Initiatives include:

- A fund for training grants for small publishers with under 26 employees, to a maximum of £400 per employee, and £2,000 per company (1994/95).
- The Foundation is offering grants to Oxford Brookes University and the Centre for Publishing Studies at Stirling University, which will enable each to offer bursaries towards the cost of course fees to a maximum of 15 students on postgraduate publishing courses who are experiencing financial hardship.
- A publishing entry scheme to assist publishers to employ graduates of publishing degree or diploma courses by contributing half of the first year's salary. Vacation work is offered to the student by the publisher concerned.

- Support is given to freelances working for their NVQs.
- A £10,000 fund to provide training grants to small independent booksellers of £150 per employee to a maximum of £500 per company. This scheme is administered by the Booksellers Association.

Chapter 6
Applying for a Job in Publishing

Introduction
You must use all your personal contacts to get an introduction. If you have none, answer advertisements or apply in writing to any firm whose list appeals to you. (The names and addresses of book publishers can be found in Whitaker's annual *Publishers in the UK and Their Addresses,* and also in *The Writers' and Artists' Yearbook* (A and C Black). Persistence is essential. Many posts are never advertised – publishers seek out likely candidates or ask their staff and contacts if they know anyone suitable. Your letter may arrive at the right moment and procure an interview.

Job Advertisements
Publishing vacancies are advertised in the *Bookseller* (Fridays, on subscription); the *Guardian* (creative and media appointments on Mondays and Saturdays); *Publishing News* (fortnightly on Fridays, on subscription); more rarely in *New Scientist* (scientific vacancies), *The Times Literary Supplement* and *The Times Educational Supplement*.

The specialist employment agencies are useful for experienced job changers; they advertise periodically in the *Bookseller*. Secretarial vacancies in publishing may be found through the *Bookseller* and the *Guardian*.

If you know or can be introduced to a member of the Publishers' Publicity Circle, and let them know you seek a job in publishing, they might be willing to place a suitable announcement on the notice board, giving your details.

The Letter of Application

Here is a list of points to remember when writing your letter of application:

- Address it to someone by name. Phone up and get a name if you do not know one.
- Remember to date and sign it, and include your address and telephone number. Print your name beneath your signature and make sure that there is an indication of your sex in the letter (if it is not evident from your name), so that the publisher knows how to address a reply.
- Mention the name of anyone likely to be known to the addressee who can speak up for you if asked for a reference.
- Keep the letter short (on one side of a good quality sheet of white A4 for preference), preferably handwritten.
- Make *absolutely sure* that there are no spelling mistakes or grammatical errors in the letter.
- If you are answering an advertisement, be sure to provide information on all the points it raises, and refer to it in your letter ('... your advertisement for an editor in the *Bookseller* of 12 February...').
- Never send out a duplicated letter; many go straight into the waste bin.
- Enclose your curriculum vitae on a separate sheet.
- Have the CV properly prepared and typed, and get some photocopies made; attach one of these to your letter.
- Keep a copy of your letter.

Your Curriculum Vitae

This should include all the following relevant details about yourself:

- Full name and address.
- Date of birth.
- Schools attended.
- Examinations passed, with grades.
- Any other honours won at school.
- Any particular position of authority held at school, eg school captain, captain of first XI, etc.
- Training courses or colleges attended and qualifications gained.
- Degree, and where obtained.

- Previous jobs held or any other experience gained.
- Software you are competent to use.
- Previous employment, if any.
- Names and addresses of two referees (other than relatives), one of whom should have personal knowledge of your capabilities.
- Personal interests, hobbies.
- Languages; if you have adequate written or speaking knowledge of any languages, mention it here.
- If you have a current driving licence, mention it here.

Telephone Application

A letter is better, but if you prefer to phone rather than write, have some written notes with you in case you are asked for information there and then. Have a copy of your curriculum vitae by you for reference.

- Try to sound pleasant, self-possessed and capable.
- Come straight to the point.
- If you are ringing from a callbox, make sure you have an ample supply of coins or, preferably, a phone card.

The Response

When you are invited to attend for interview, allow time for the journey and add a margin for contingencies. If you are not familiar with the area, ask exactly where the office is in relation to the nearest tube station, bus stop or parking space and try to fit in a dummy run beforehand. If you are applying for an editorial vacancy, you may be asked to do a test or be given a test paper to take away. It will probably consist of a passage to edit or proof-read, carefully designed to reveal your general knowledge, style, grammar, spelling and punctuation.

The Interview

Points to remember
- Be on time.
- Make sure you are well-groomed.
- Smile pleasantly and look directly at the interviewer.
- Speak clearly without mumbling.
- Don't smoke.

- Try to avoid bald 'yes' and 'no' answers, but don't ramble.
- Remember all the time that you have to sell yourself to the employer. Concentrate on your good points and abilities, rather than what you can't do.
- Always be lively and enthusiastic.

Questions to be prepared for
- What made you decide you wanted a career in publishing?
- Why did you apply for this job?
- What makes you think you will be good at it?
- How would you like your career to develop?

Take examples of any relevant work you have done.

Accepting a Job

Before you get your contract of employment, before you even write a letter of acceptance, you should make sure you know your position. No one should accept a job without understanding what the job entails, what your hours and rate of pay are and the holiday entitlement. If you have any doubts or queries, now is the time to clear them up.

Contract of Employment

A contract of employment exists as soon as someone offers you a job (even verbally) at a certain rate of pay and you accept. Within eight weeks of your starting work the employer is required by law to give you written details of your contract. These include:

- Job title.
- Pay.
- How you are paid.
- Hours of work.
- Holiday entitlement and pay.
- Length of notice.
- Disciplinary and grievance procedures.
- Pension rights.

The contract of employment is a legal document, so make sure that you keep it in a safe place.

Temporary or Vacation Work

This may be available during rush periods. It is important to take *any* opportunity of working, even if the firm or the job is not what you wanted, or the pay is poor. You will be enlarging your experience *and* making contacts; through such contacts new job opportunities often arise. A temporary job during the vacation can lead to a permanent post when your course is over and will add authority to your CV.

Chapter 7
Further Reading

Ball, Linda (1992) *Careers in Art and Design*, 6th edn, Kogan Page
Baverstock, Alison (1993) *Are Books Different? Marketing in The Book Trade*, Kogan Page
Baverstock, Alison (1993) *How to Market Books*, revised edn, Kogan Page
Breckman, Malcolm (1988) *Starting and Running a Bookshop* (Malcolm Breckman, 2 Vines Avenue, London N3 2QD)
Brown, Iain D et al (1991) *The Young Publishers' Handbook*, Society of Young Publishers
Butcher, Judith (1992) *Copy-Editing: The Cambridge Handbook*, 3rd edn, Cambridge University Press
Clark, Charles (1993) *Publishing Agreements: A Book of Precedents*, 4th edn, Butterworth
Clark, Giles N (1994) *Inside Book Publishing: A Career Builder's Guide*, 2nd edn, Blueprint
Evans, Hilary (1979) *The Art of Picture Research*, David and Charles
Evans, Hilary, ed (1986) *The Picture Researcher's Handbook*, 3rd edn, Van Nostrand Reinhold
Foster Charles (1993) *Editing, Design and Book Production*, Pluto
Godber, Bill, Webb R and Smith, K (1992) *Marketing for Small Publishers*, 2nd edn, Pluto
Hird, Caroline (1993) *Careers in Marketing, Advertising and Public Relations*, 5th edn, Kogan Page
Legat, Michael (1991) *An Author's Guide to Publishing*, revised edn, Hale
Medina, Peter and Donald, V (1994) *Careers in Journalism*, 6th edn, Kogan Page
Miller, Ian (1993) *Successful Bookselling*, Book House Training Centre/UNESCO
Stewart, Dorothy M (1987) *Bluff Your Way in Publishing*, Ravette
Turner, Barry, *Writer's Handbook*, annual, Macmillan

Chapman and Hall publish excellent titles for publishers under the Blueprint list.
The following reference books are also recommended:

The Oxford Dictionary for Writers and Editors, Oxford University Press, 1981
Directory of Book Publishers, Distributors and Wholesalers, Booksellers Association, annual
Directory of Booksellers Association Members, Booksellers Association, annual
Hart's Rules for Compositors and Readers at the University Press, Oxford, 39th edn, Oxford University Press, 1983
Publishers in the UK and Their Addresses, Whitaker, annual
The Writers' and Artists' Yearbook, A and C Black, annual.

Other tools of the trade include dictionaries, atlases, encyclopaedias, dictionaries of quotations, gazetteers, *Brewer's Dictionary of Phrase and Fable*, and thesauruses.

Chapter 8
Useful Addresses

Administrative, Clerical, Technical and Supervisory (ACTS)
Transport and General Workers' Union, Transport House, Smith Square, London SW1P 3JB; 071-828 7788

Andrea Marks PR
Laburnum House, Spring Villa Road, Edgware, Middlesex HA8 7EB; 081-951 5441

Association of Authors' Agents
c/o Nicky Kennedy, 5th Floor, The Chambers, Chelsea Harbour, London SW10 0XF; 071-351 4763

Association of Learned and Professional Society Publishers
48 Kelsey Lane, Beckenham, Kent BR3 3NE; 081-658 0459

BA Training
Booksellers Association of Great Britain and Ireland,
272 Vauxhall Bridge Road, London SW1V 1BA; 071-834 5477

Book House Training Centre
Book House, 45 East Hill, London SW18 2QZ; 081-874 2718/4608

The *Bookseller*
12 Dyott Street, London WC1A 1DF; 071-836 8911

Booksellers Association of Great Britain and Ireland, *see* BA Training above

British Association of Industrial Editors
3 Locks Yard, High Street, Sevenoaks, Kent TN13 1LT; 0732 459331

The British Library Centre for the Book
Great Russell Street, London WC1B 3DG; 071-323 7608

British Printing Industries Federation
11 Bedford Row, London WC1R 4DX; 071-242 6904

Broadcast Entertainment Cinematograph Theatre Union (BECTU)
111 Wardour Street, London W1V 4AY; 071-437 8506

Business and Technology Education Council
Central House, Upper Woburn Place, London WC1H 0HE; 071-413 8400

Chapterhouse
2 Southernhay West, Exeter, Devon EX1 1JG; 0392 499488

Chartered Institute of Marketing (CIM)
Moor Hall, Cookham, Maidenhead, Berkshire SL6 9QH; 0628 524922

Chartered Society of Designers
29 Bedford Square, London WC1B 3EG; 071-631 1510

Frances Lincoln Ltd
Apollo Works, 5 Charlton Kings Road, London NW5 2SB; 071-284 4009

Freelance MS
PO Box 572, Bournemouth, Dorset B4 9YA

Institute of Scientific and Technical Communicators
King's Court, 2-16 Goodge Street, London W1P 1FF; 071-436 4425

London Institute, Professional Development Unit
London College of Printing and Distributive Trades,
Elephant and Castle, London SE1 6SB; 071-735 0810/793 0077

London School of Publishing
86 Old Brompton Road, South Kensington, London SW7 3LQ; 071-584 4070

Middlesex University, Small Press Centre
White Hart Lane, London N17 8HR; 081-362 6058

National Extension College
18 Brooklands Avenue, Cambridge CB2 2HN; 0223 316644

National Union of Journalists (Book Branch)
Acorn House, 314-320 Gray's Inn Road, London WC1X 8DP; 071-278 7916

Open University
Walton Hall, Milton Keynes MK7 6AG; 0908 653231

Oxford Publicity Partnership
36 Lonsdale Road, Summertown, Oxford OX2 7EW; 0865 53032

Oxford Women in Publishing
c/o Training Matters, 15 Pitts Road, Headington Quarry, Oxford OX3 8BA; 0865 66964

Password Training
23 New Mount Street, Manchester M4 4DE; 061-953 4009

Paul Hamlyn Foundation
Sussex House, 12 Upper Mall, London W6 9TA; 081-741 2812

Publishers Association
19 Bedford Square, London WC1B 3HJ; 071-580 6321

Publishers Publicity Circle
48 Crabtree Lane, London SW6 6LW; 071-385 3708

Publishing News
43 Museum Street, London WC1A 1LY; 071-404 0304

Publishing Qualifications Board
344–354 Gray's Inn Road, London WC1X 8BP; 071-278 4411

Rapid Results College
Tuition House, 27–37 St George's Road, London SW19 4DS; 081-947 7272

Scottish Vocational Education Council (SCOTVEC)
24 Douglas Street, Glasgow G2 7NQ; 041-248 7900

Society of Freelance Editors and Proofreaders
38 Rochester Road, London NW1 9JJ; 071-813 3113

Society of Indexers
38 Rochester Road, London NW1 9JJ; 071-916 7809

Society of Picture Researchers and Editors
c/o Patricia Leigh, The Financial Times, 1 Southwark Bridge, London SE1 9HL; 071-873 3000

Society of Young Publishers
c/o J Whitaker & Sons Ltd, 12 Dyott Street, London WC1A 1DF; 071-836 8911

Training Matters
15 Pitts Road, Headington Quarry, Oxford OX3 8BA; 0865 66964

Translators Association
Society of Authors, 84 Drayton Gardens, London SW10 9SB; 071-373 6642

UK Serials Group
114 Woodstock Road, Witney, Oxfordshire OX8 6DY; 0993 703466

Women in Publishing
c/o J Whitaker & Sons Ltd, 12 Dyott Street, London WC1A 1DF; 071-836 8911

The Kogan Page Careers Series

This series consists of short guides (96–144 pages) to different careers for school and college leavers, graduates and anyone wanting to start anew. Each book serves as an introduction to a particular career and to jobs available within that field, including details of training qualifications and courses. The following 'Careers in' titles are available in paperback. Enquiries phone 071-278 0433.

Accountancy (*5th edition*)
Architecture (*3rd edition*)
Art and Design (*6th edition*)
Catering and Hotel Management (*4th edition*)
Environmental Conservation (*5th edition*)
Fashion (*3rd edition*)
Film and Video (*3rd edition*)
Hairdressing and Beauty Therapy (*6th edition*)
Journalism (*6th edition*)
The Law (*6th edition*)
Marketing, Advertising and Public Relations (*5th edition*)
Medicine, Dentistry and Mental Health (*6th edition*)
Nursing and Related Professions (*6th edition*)
Police Force (*4th edition*)
Publishing and Bookselling (*2nd edition*)
Retailing (*4th edition*)
Secretarial and Office Work (*6th edition*)
Social Work (*5th edition*)
Sport (*5th edition*)
Teaching (*5th edition*)
Television and Radio (*5th edition*)
The Theatre (*4th edition*)
Travel Industry (*4th edition*)
Using Languages (*6th edition*)
Working Outdoors (*5th edition*)
Working with Animals (*6th edition*)
Working with Children and Young People (*6th edition*)

Also Available from Kogan Page

Great Answers to Tough Interview Questions: How to Get the Job You Want (3rd edition), Martin John Yate (1992)

How to Get on in Marketing, Advertising and Public Relations: A Career Development Guide (2nd edition), ed Norman Hart and Norman Waite (1994)

How to Pass Graduate Recruitment Tests, Mike Bryon (1994)

How to Pass Selection Tests, Mike Bryon and Sanjay Modha (1991)

How to Succeed in A Levels (2nd edition), Howard Barlow (1991)

How to Win as a Part-time Student, Tom Bourner and Phil Race (1990)

How You Can Get that Job!: Application Forms and Letters Made Easy, Rebecca Corfield (1992)

Making it in Sales: A Career Guide for Women, Mary J Foster with Timothy R V Foster (1993)

Manage Your Own Career, Ben Ball (1989)

Preparing Your Own CV, Rebecca Corfield (1990)

Successful Interview Skills, Rebecca Corfield (1992)

Technical Selection Tests and How to Pass Them, Mike Bryon and Sanjay Modha (1993)

Test Your Own Aptitude (2nd edition), Jim Barrett and Geoff Williams (1990)

Your First Job (2nd edition), Vivien Donald and Ray Grose (1993)